BLACK RESISTANCE
BEFORE THE CIVIL WAR

William F. Cheek

Associate Professor
Department of History
San Diego State College

GLENCOE PRESS
A Division of The Macmillan Company
Beverly Hills, California
Collier-Macmillan Ltd., London

To Aimee Lee

GLENCOE PRESS
A Division of The Macmillan Company
8701 Wilshire Boulevard
Beverly Hills, California 90211
Collier-Macmillan Canada, Ltd., Toronto, Canada

Library of Congress catalog card number: 74-104865

First printing, 1970

Contents

The right of man to the enjoyment of freedom is a settled point; and where he is deprived of this, without any criminal act of his own, it is his duty to regain his liberty at every cost.
—WILLIAM WELLS BROWN, *The Black Man*, 1863

Preface

Not so long ago I was invited to an almost all black high school in San Diego to deliver a lecture on some aspects of black American history. I chose to talk about black resistance: the sabotage efforts, the labor strikes, the barn burnings by black slaves that reappear again and again in the plantation records, in the personal reminiscences of ex-slaves and foreign travelers, and in Northern and Southern newspapers alike. I spoke of "General" Gabriel and Denmark Vesey and Nat Turner, genuine black revolutionaries out of the American past. I called attention to David Walker and the Reverend Henry Highland Garnet, two Northern black men who, more than a hundred years ago, advocated that slaves rise up and kill their masters if the latter refused to free them.

When I had finished and the auditorium was nearly cleared, one black student came up to me and asked, hurt obvious in her voice, "Why weren't we told all this before now?" I mumbled, "You know the answer to that better than I"; and she walked away, nodding affirmatively. Then it was a white student's turn. "I guess black people know all that about their past," he volunteered. "But why haven't we been told about it?"

The questions posed by these two students, one black and one white, both kept in the dark all these years, take the measurement of our current predicament. Our orientation in this country has been "divine right white." Our society, as we are now being repeatedly reminded, is indeed racist, but this racism is not altogether deliberate or malicious. Some of it stems from our ignorance and misconceptions about the black man in American history.

Here the historian has been just as guilty as others. Betrayed by his own values, he has written history (there are, of course, the excep-

---

(NOTE. — The punctuation, and sometimes the capitalization, of documents in this book has been altered to make them more understandable to students who are not used to older typographical styles. In no case has wording been changed without the use of brackets to show editorial additions, and the footnotes indicate which selections have been altered typographically. It is presumed that students will go to the original sources if they wish to study documents exactly as they were first written or printed; these sources are all identified in footnotes.)

tions) from a white-superiority perspective, often without thinking very much about it. Only with the changes brought about in the age of civil rights and after has the historian, generally speaking, altered his long-held assumption that the black man is inferior and therefore his role in American history has been inferior.

Nowhere is our ignorance more appalling or, perhaps, more dangerous than in our viewing the black American as an Uncle Tom. As recently as September of 1968, according to a Louis Harris poll, the majority of the American people interviewed conceived of the Negro as essentially lazy, shiftless, easy-going, given to acceptance of his lot.

Even a superficial reading of American history will give anyone serious cause for re-evaluating this stereotype. Indeed, one of the major themes in black American history has been that of resistance, Uncle Tom itself being merely one of its many forms.

Believing that it is what we do not know about black history that is hurting us all, I propose in the essay and documents that follow to examine various aspects of black resistance before the Civil War.

I wish to thank my two co-conspirators, Maribeth Spearmon, who traveled, and compiled, and typed, and cared, and Aimee Lee Cheek, who typed, and edited, and rewrote, and loved.

William F. Cheek
July, 1969

Chapter One

Introductory Essay

A central theme in black American history has been that of resistance. Contrary to popular thinking, resistance did not spring up, full-grown and unparalleled, in the civil rights and black power movements of the 1960's; rather, it is deeply rooted in the American and African past, beginning with the beginnings of the slave trade itself. When black people were torn from their homes in the African interior or along the coastal waters, they resisted. When black people were torturously transported to the New World, they resisted. When subsequently black people were enslaved and forced to toil for Northern and Southern masters, they resisted. And when black people were compelled to live out their lives under the severe discrimination that obtained across the pre–Civil War North, they resisted.

This is not to say that every black man, behind a grinning Sambo mask, was only a slightly toned-down version of Nat Turner, always at the ready to deal out death and destruction to his oppressor. Nor is it reasonable to assume that slaves occupied most of their waking moments sabotaging those responsible for their lowly status, or that free Negroes, North or South, preached and plotted black liberation without letup. In reality, black revolutionaries were rare, for true revolutionaries come seldom in history; and when it comes to estimating how many blacks, North or South, had the courage, persistence, and resourcefulness to resist in less spectacular if perhaps more effective ways than revolt, of course it is impossible to say. Yet resistance is not a matter of numbers merely, or even most importantly, but rather a matter of the spirit; and it was a spirit that burned fiercely in black people. Black people, like all other subjugated peoples throughout history, have never placidly acquiesced in the cruel assortment of brutalities, incivilities, and injustices that have been inflicted upon them. The ways they found to confront, counteract or rebuff these oppressions were both physical and psychological, ranging in each from the crude and violent to the subtle and nonviolent, varying in form from the fight with the overseer to the telling of a tale about Brer Rabbit.

SECTION 1. THE CONDITION OF SLAVERY

At every stage of the Atlantic slave trade, which persisted from 1518 to possibly as late as 1880, having been initiated and continued because it was lucrative to both Europeans and Africans, physical opposition to enslavement manifested itself. After seizure in a village war or kidnapping raid by African chieftains, blacks had to be march-driven from the interior, their necks and arms firmly trussed, and, upon arrival at the West African coastline where they awaited sale to the European trader, they sometimes attempted to strangle themselves in the chains that bound them. Pending departure the captives were penned in temporary slave houses constructed on ships' decks or in barracoons or stockades on shore, lest they escape — which they consistently attempted to do, now and again successfully. Recurrently, slaves flung themselves into the shark-patrolled waters, where if they were not devoured, they often drowned.

On board ship, the Africans continued their efforts to free them-selves, sometimes through mass uprisings while ships lay at anchor or, less often, on the high seas. Accounts of well over one hundred and fifty slave mutinies survive. Mutinies were especially prevalent on British ships after 1750 when as a result of the dissolution of the Royal African Company the slave trade fell wholly into the hands of independent businessmen who, to maximize a profit, took fewer pre-cautions and hired on fewer crewmen.

Together with the longing for liberation, special considerations prompted shipboard revolts. Periodic epidemics that weakened the crew rendered the slave ship peculiarly vulnerable to attack by the imprisoned, who were driven to desperation by inhuman physical-psychological conditions, for slaves commonly were manacled together, wrist-to-wrist, ankle-to-ankle, and packed into a disease-rife hold, so confining as to make sitting upright impossible. An added element, and a terrifying one, was the generalized belief among many blacks that the enslaver intended to cannibalize them.

Slaves proved resourceful in exploiting any opportunity that arose. Women, who were allowed more run of the deck than men, sometimes managed to snatch up unattended arms and ammunition and thus precipitate an armed struggle. The small tubs used for eating served, in one instance, for beating the captain to death. On another occasion, a crude hammer that had been fashioned on a ship's anchor doubling as an anvil was discovered in time to avert a similar episode. Abortive mutinies unfailingly left ruinous scars: a partially gutted ship, mutila tion for some slaves and ship's crewmen, death for others. In their broadly researched and crisply written book on the Atlantic slave trade, Black Cargoes,* Mannix and Cowley, noting that after successful uprisings the ship often was steered to shore, looted, and demolished, estimate that one out of ten mutinies in African waters resulted in destruction of the crew.

Where powerless to effect a mutiny, many Africans resorted to suicide. It was not unheard-of for a knot of blacks to summon up enough strength to snap their chains and hurl themselves overboard, "exulting with apparent glee," according to one report, as they disappeared beneath the waters. Aboard the English ship Brookes, one slave, having been thwarted twice in his attempts to slash his own throat, ceased eating and shortly after died of hunger. Self-inflicted starvation was, in fact, such a common practice among the slaves that a special compulsory feeding contraption, the speculum oris (mouth opener) became standard equipment on a slaver. Yet another cruel appetite-stimulant was a shovel of hot coals applied near the victim's lips. But the hunger suicides persisted. Moreover, certain strong-willed slaves, helped toward death, perhaps, by extreme shock or the numerous diseases arising from filthy ship conditions, simply fell into what was called "fixed melancholy," and gave up their lives.

Even at the port of sale, captains were by no means assured of their human cargo. In 1807 two boatloads of slaves, rather than accept their

---

* See the bibliography at the end of this chapter for references to all books cited.

destiny, starved themselves to death in Charleston harbor. And when the *Prince of Orange* put in at St. Kitts some years later, more than one hundred men jumped into the sea, thirty-three to be drowned. At the marketplace itself, slaves sometimes broke for their freedom. It was the less-than-honest captain who ever used the phrase, "smooth sailing," to describe his slaving enterprise.

Englishmen, with the Portuguese and Spanish as their example, began transporting black people involuntarily to the English colonies early in the seventeenth century. Dispute persists, and probably can never be satisfactorily resolved, as to the black man's earliest status, servant or slave, in this country. It is definite, however, that by 1700 he was a slave, viewed in law and most often treated in fact as a chattel, a piece of personal property, any damage to which by another party could result in a court case for trespass.

In the North slavery survived until the period immediately following the Revolution, at which time libertarian impulses combined with economic considerations to abolish it. During the existence of Northern slavery, despite laws and treatment somewhat less harsh than found in the South, slaves resisted in numerous ways: by running away, stealing the master's possessions, firing ships, warehouses, and homes, committing acts of murder and mutilation as well as sex crimes, and, finally, participating in insurrection.

Across the South slavery, numbering four million in its ranks by the eve of the Civil War, was very much alive. While the humanitarian winds of the western world swirled around it, the South resolutely upheld its peculiar institution. Not only did slavery bring economic profits (according to most scholars), but it also furnished crucial support to the region's social system. Slavery helped satisfy, as it stimulated, the power-status-prestige drives of the slaveholder. Moreover, masters kept slaves for reasons of race. Thus, the black man was debased because he was perceived as different — less aggressive than the white man, savage, heathen, and black, the very color itself setting off a negative emotional charge. Finally, the South paid strong allegiance to the institution of slavery out of fear — of the slave and of what he might do if he were freed.

By no means was the slave system static or frozen; on the contrary, it was marked by a seemingly endless variety of forms. The fluctuations of the economy were particularly influential in determining the treatment of the slave, often harsh under boom conditions but more relaxed and paternalistic once the tempo of economic life had slowed.

The number of slaves on a plantation, the proportion of blacks to whites in a particular area, the degree of fear in a given community, and the constantly alternating currents within local, state, and national politics — all helped to determine the particular form of slavery in a given area. Variations also resulted from the type of employment given the slave. Thus, the system discriminated in favor of house Negroes and slave-drivers over field hands, as it also favored skilled over unskilled workers. Further, slaves who worked in cities, in factories, along the river, and in laboratories had somewhat more freedom of action and status than those who labored in the fields.

However, even allowing for the most benevolent of masters and propitious of circumstances, still the slave was denied the right to live as a man. Each area of his existence was defined by the rigorous slave codes, designed to give legal sanction to the superior white and inferior black roles in the society, that disciplined both white and black Southerners. The slaveholder, with all but absolute power bestowed on him, was allotted certain obligations. He was expected to train the slave to mirror the master's values and to submit completely to the master's will. The slave, as a chattel, could not hold property or exercise any civil or political rights. Born a slave, he would remain a slave, unless his master or a governmental authority elected to free him, and he would pass on this status to his children.

The law also enjoined the slaveowner to care for the needs of the slave and deal with him humanely. How the slaveholder defined and carried out this obligation can be speculated upon, in part, from the calculations of a scholar who estimated the average cost of maintaining a slave in the ante-bellum South at about twenty-one dollars a year. It is not difficult to understand how costs were kept low. The slave's food, distributed weekly, consisted of a peck of corn and a few pounds of salt pork or bacon, perhaps supplemented (if the slaveholder allowed it) by vegetables grown after regular work hours in a small garden, and occasionally by meats from the smokehouse or kitchen which he acquired by stealing, or "taking," as the slave called it. Former bondsman Austin Steward was doubtless expressing a widespread sentiment when he bitterly remarked of his master that "no slave of his is ever likely to suffer from the gout, superinduced by excessive high living." As for clothing, the slave received a minimally adequate summer and winter issue; shoes came in two sizes, large and small. His house usually had one room and a dirt floor and was built of logs, with little in the way of sanitation or safety features. One ex-slave said his house had "so many cracks in it that when I would sleep . . . I could lie in bed and count the stars through the cracks." In such an environment disease flourished, with especially high mortality rates among infants and new mothers. The slaveholder, who relied mainly on folk remedies to cure his ailing bondsmen, kept medical expenses to a minimum. Care for the aged was scarcely a concern, despite all the affectionate stories told by senti- mental white Southerners about "old uncles," for the life expectancy of a male field hand did not extend beyond thirty years of age.

If the many faceted master–slave relationship fostered a certain aristocratic grace and charm in the Southern planter, often commented upon by travelers and other contemporaries, it evoked at the same time the violent and sadistic aspects of his nature. If one is to judge from the evidence of many slave narratives, the most common form of com- munication from master (or overseer) to slave was physical punishment. Even allowing for the tendency of ex-slaves to exaggerate the brutality of the system in order to engage antislavery sympathies, the testimony of Austin Steward was probably not far off the mark when he noted that "no slave could possibly escape being punished — I care not how attentive they might be, nor how industrious — punished they must be, and punished they were." While a slave was seldom beaten so severely that he would not be able to walk to the fields the next day, thirty-nine lashes, and more, "well laid on," were more often reality than legend. In the consciousness of many a slave, the earliest memory involved a whipping.

More damaging than physical brutality was the punishment inflicted upon the mind and spirit. The great nineteenth-century black leader, Frederick Douglass, observed that "slavery does away with fathers, as it does away with families." The male slave, who endured the common humiliation of being referred to as "Ann's Tom," living in "Ann's cabin," was forbidden to fill the provider-protector role. He had little control over the sale or punishment of any family member, nor over the sexual violation of his women, whether for the white man's pleasure or for purposes of breeding. One former slave commented that "the hardest thing in slavery is not the work — it is the abuse of a man, and, in my case, of a man's wife and children." The female slave, who like the man suffered the degrading self-knowledge that she was valued primarily for the amount of work she could perform, bore the additional burden of being sexually vulnerable to the whim of any white male. Then, too, as the house slave was required to care for the home and children of the owners and help the white mistress at her toilet, so she was denied the opportunity to care for her own home and children and to enhance her own beauty. The woman who worked in the fields, as most women did, had even less chance to develop her femininity.

Forbidden by law to learn to read and write, frequently discouraged from developing a spiritual life, wounded emotionally by the lack of love and hope and the prevalence of hate and fear, the slave found it extraordinarily difficult to build the kind of positive identity that is essential to a sane and peaceful adjustment to the world. So the slave, man and woman, was often not sane or peaceful but irrational and violent. But then, so was his world.

Slaveholders, in their writings and orations, or when queried by Northern or foreign guests, unfailingly characterized their slaves as happy "niggers" with happy problems, and on cue, with the owner close by, slaves went through the motions of appearing supremely con tented with their lot. The false show of cheerful docility fooled a few, but both master and slave really knew better. Master and slave knew, as the common sense of the matter, what Frederick Douglass as a slave child realized as early as seven or eight. "I distinctly remember," Douglass wrote, "being, even then, most strongly impressed with the idea of being a freeman some day. This cheering assurance was an inborn dream of my human nature — a constant menace to slavery — and one which all the powers of slavery were unable to silence or extinguish."

Slaves, even the most dull witted ones, had ample exposure to the ideas and symbols of freedom. Besides observing the freedom of the white man and his family daily, they might accompany them on such special occasions as Fourth of July celebrations, attending while the Declaration of Independence was honored. An ex-slave recalled, "I listened with great wonder to the Texas orators, as they talked about liberty. I thought it might be as good for me as for others."

Another testified that the more slaves knew of freedom, the more they coveted it. Ex-slave Solomon Northup wrote: "Let them know the heart of the poor slave — learn his secret thoughts — thoughts he dare not utter in the hearing of the white man; let them sit by him in the silent watches of the night — converse with him in trustful confidence, of 'life, liberty, and the pursuit of happiness'; and they will find that ninety-nine out of every hundred are intelligent enough to understand their situation, and to cherish in their bosoms the love of freedom, as passionately as themselves."

Partially because the Southerner did strongly value his own independence besides paying frequent lip service to it, he was all the more aware, consciously or unconsciously, of similar strivings for freedom in his slaves; and he knew what terrible consequences those strivings, if somehow developed into action, could have for him. Insurrection was the single idea guaranteed to send shockwaves through the entire Southland. The masters, wrote the former slave Lewis Clarke, "live in constant fear upon this subject [insurrection]. The least unusual noise at night alarms them greatly. They cry out, 'What is that?' 'Are the boys all in?' "

Actually, the master–slave–plantation complex itself militated against rebellion. By comparison with the slave economies in the West Indies and Brazil, where revolts were regular occurrences, the South was characterized by the relatively great distances between plantations and the relatively modest units of production. Such a situation made it difficult to assemble large groups of slaves for the purpose of organizing, planning, and then carrying out an insurrection.

The same geographical and economic setup, as David Brion Davis has observed, doubtless played a part in making the Southern master–slave affiliation more flexible than it was under the West Indian slave system. The very insecurity of their position, surrounded as they were by their bondsmen, made slaveholders adept at devising an elaborate and sophisticated strategy of divide-and-conquer. Intimacy among slaves was discouraged. Frequently, kinship groupings were disrupted. Poor communication was further insured by gathering on a plantation slaves who spoke different African languages. And, to exaserbate matters even more, owners seeded the fields and slave quarters with spies. Douglass learned quite early that you "trust no man" and that "a still tongue makes a wise head." The nature of the institution was such that betrayal was precipitated, as a former slave noted, by the desire "to get a new coat, or two or three dollars."

The master insisted that the various cultures black men brought with them be replaced by a culture of subservience. If the slave sought recognition and approval, these had to come from his master. What power a slave achieved, what identity he had were defined by the master.

So many slaves scrambled to do the chance bidding of their owner. "Few privileges were esteemed higher, by the slaves of the out-farms," Frederick Douglass wrote, "than that of being selected to do errands at the Great House Farm. It was associated in their minds with greatness." Josiah Henson, another ex-slave, remarked that "one word of commendation from the petty despot who ruled over us would set me up for a month."

The lord of the manor did not have to be an expert psychologist to recognize the overwhelming need for many safety valves if he were to head off violent explosions from the servant of the quarters. Rewards, as a consequence, were plentiful enough. In addition to the special status mentioned above, slaves sometimes were permitted to hold religious services, have a garden, or hire themselves out for wages. Slaves were invited to overeat, romp and kick up their dancing heels on holidays, especially Christmas, when, according to Douglass, it was a "disgrace not to get drunk." Henry Bibb, like Douglass a former slave, added that whites "go among the slaves and give them whiskey to see them dance, 'pat juber,' sing and play the banjo. Then get them to wrestling, fighting, jumping, running foot races and butting each other like sheep."

As effectively as they prevented unity among their slaves, masters built an awesome solidarity among themselves. The slave codes proved the necessary cohesive instrument, each planter recognizing that the laws were the principal deterrent force to large-scale uprisings. These laws varied from place to place, characteristically being most stringent in areas where blacks greatly outnumbered whites, but certain general features predominated. Slaves could not be educated. Slaves could not leave the plantation without permission; they could not come together in large numbers; they were forbidden to bear arms or to strike a white man.

In many areas white men (frequently nonslaveholders) were obligated by law to watch over the community's safety by serving in a slave patrol. Additionally, city and state police and militia forces and the United States Army were readily available. The blitzkrieg-like efficiency of the white police powers during the Denmark Vesey and Nat Turner revolts in particular, in combination with the bloody vengeance wreaked on the black populace following slave outbreaks — men and women struck down, often indiscriminately, bodies strung up in chains, heads sliced and rammed onto poles at public places — informed the slave quite clearly of the penalty for revolt.

How many slave rebellions actually occurred, despite all of this, is open to question. In his ambitious and in many ways admirable American Negro Slave Revolts, Herbert Aptheker stakes a claim for two hundred and fifty slave insurrections and conspiracies in American history. More recently, Winthrop Jordan, in a masterful study of race relations (and much else) titled *White Over Black,* has suggested that the number was probably not over a dozen. On the evidence presented, some of Aptheker's revolts do appear to be little more than labor protests, strikes, and, perhaps most commonly, white fantasies jarred loose by raw fear. What constituted a rumor and what constituted a conspiracy was, and is, in many instances, impossible to determine.

Of the slave revolts that can be authenticated, none succeeded in the United States. The system was never in any real danger of upheaval, a fact understood by the great majority of those slaves who reflected on the matter at all, and who therefore never seriously involved themselves in revolt. Most slaves probably felt like Solomon Northup, who admitted that while a bondsman, "more than once" he had "joined in serious conversation about insurrection," but that he saw only "certain defeat and death" as the result, and so desisted. Resistance in the form of a collective effort to destroy the system was almost certainly a suicide mission.

Comprehending the power of his oppressor but feeling the hardness of his life, repelled by slavery and attracted to freedom, the slave endured, yet with an emotional tension that demanded release. He relieved this pain, frequently if he tended to be aggressive by nature, and less often if he were more passive, by various methods of resistance, fighting back at the master day by day, sometimes spontaneously but often with premeditation, and thereby holding on to some measure of dignity. Thus, he fled. He sabotaged. He delayed. He deceived. He stole. He murdered. He revolted.

And, perhaps most remarkably, he created his own art. In spite of the humiliations and intimidations, the European and American cultural impositions, and, indeed, all the many deliberate efforts to destroy his separate identity, the black man under slavery managed to develop an independent and distinctive Afro-American culture, the strength of which was reflected in its humor, folklore, poetry, language, song, and religion.

Just as the creation and maintenance of this culture was in itself an act of resistance, so, threading through the materials, is the theme of confronting the master. A contemporary black scholar, Mike Thelwell, argues that the "central impulse" of the language of slavery was "survival and resistance." Because the references to outdoing or fooling or injuring the white man had to be oblique, for fear the master would discover the slave's true feeling, the language characteristically was subtle. Only in situations comfortably private, or with an unusually tolerant master, did the allusions become more direct.

An example of the folk wit of the slave quarters was supplied by an ex-slave in a story he related to interviewers of the New Deal Federal Writer's Project. A slave killed one of the master's pigs and the master, spying him, inquired what animal he had. The slave replied, "A possum." The master looked and saw it was a shoat, whereupon the slave, realizing he had been found out, declared, "Master, it may be a shoat now, but it sure was a possum while ago when I put 'im in the sack." The tale demonstrates how a slave manipulated his words in order to appear inoffensive and humorous, while he was really taking advantage of the white man.

By way of contrast, ex-slave Peter Randolph in his autobiography reveals the slave's talent for satire in a strikingly undisguised form.

> This slaveholder was a great fighter (as most of them are), and had prepared himself for the contest with greatest care, and wished to know how he looked; so he said, "Pompey, how do I look?" "Oh, massa, *mighty*!" "What do you mean by 'mighty,' Pompey?" "Why, massa, you look noble." "What do you mean by 'noble'?" "Why, sar, you look just like one *lion*." "Why, Pompey, where have you ever seen a lion?" "I seen one down in yonder field the other day, massa." "Pompey, you foolish fellow, that was a jackass." "Was it, massa? Well, you look just like him."

The myths and folktales created or adapted by slaves frequently reflected attitudes of resistance. Popular among the blacks themselves were the stories of Old John, the slave who by virtue of his quick wits repeatedly made his master appear foolish. Better known generally are the Brer Rabbit tales. Read on one level, through white glasses, they chronicle the adventures of a sly, "mischievous" rabbit, as he skirmishes day after day with the more powerful but comparatively dull-witted wolf, fox, and bear; but from the perspective of the slave quarters, these charming animal folk take on quite different roles. The slave identified himself with the rabbit, one of nature's weakest animals, while the white man was seen as the wolf, fox, and bear, three of the strongest and most vicious creatures. He depicted their society, the master's *milieu*, as violent, rapacious, hypocritical, and sex-driven.

In the Brer Rabbit tales the world is turned upside down. Not only does Brer Rabbit triumph over his three enemies, he personally has a hand in causing the violent death of each one. In Southern taboo black men may never eat with white; Brer Rabbit so terrorizes the animal community that they are finally forced to bring him to their table to partake of a communal meal. In Southern taboo black men may never take white women; Brer Rabbit bests his rivals for female favors and demonstrates superior sexual potency time and again. In the antebellum South men vied, above all, for power and prestige; in the allegorical South of slave folklore, Brer Rabbit takes these prizes for his own.

Secular folk rhymes were variously referred to as devil tunes, fiddle songs, cornfield hollers, and jig-tunes. In one rhyme, the slave betrayer was scored thusly:

> Dar is old Uncle Billy, he's a mighty good Nigger.
> He tote all de news to Mosser a little bigger.
> When you tells Uncle Billy, You wants free fer a fac';
> De nex' day de hide drap off'n yo' back.

The white man's religion was satirized in a parody of the Lord's Prayer:

> "Our Fader, Which art in heaben!" — —
> White man owe me leben and pay me seben.
> "D'y kingdom come! D'y will be done!" — —
> An' if I hadn' tuck dat, I wouldn' git none.

The personal appearance of Mossa was itself subject for ridicule:

> When dey gits old and gray
> When dey gits old and gray
> White folks look like monkeys
> When dey gits old and gray.

In spirituals, the slave's religious music, he achieved his greatest facility in shaping a language of ironic intentions. By regulating his physical gestures, cadence, and intonation, the songs came out one way for the white man's ears and quite another for the slave's. Several levels of meaning could be built into the spiritual. Negro writer J. Saunders Redding has noted that "Swing Low, Sweet Chariot" and "Git on Board, Little Chillen" "might at one time be a call to a religious service, at another a message telling of a successful escape, or at still another an announcement of the imminence of an underground conductor." The master, hearing the lines "O Canaan, Sweet Canaan, I am bound for the land of Canaan," would naturally think the singer was longing for the Biblical promised land or Heaven. The slave, however, knew

Canaan as the code name for Canada for, as Douglass said, the "North was our Canaan." Similarly, in the spirituals Egypt stood for the South, the Pharoah was the master, Moses the slave leader, and the Israelites the slaves themselves.

Through spirituals, which white Southerners considered songs of contentment or yearnings for a heavenly world, slaves revealed their innermost feelings: joy and lamentation, protest and resistance. To Frederick Douglass, spirituals "told a tale of woe; they breathed the prayer and complaint of souls boiling over with the bitterest anguish. Every tone was a testimony against slavery, and a prayer to God for deliverance from chains." One of the very significant black contributions to American life, the spiritual, in some of its forms, can be regarded as the slave's musical declaration of independence.

Like the spiritual, the slave's entire religious observance was subject to opposing interpretations. If permitted by the master and supervised by him (in South Carolina blacks were forbidden by law to hold religious services, as they were, sometimes by law and sometimes by custom, in other areas), the religious service seemed to strongly emphasize obedience and focus on the promise of a hereafter. In fact, numerous slaves did hold to this kind of faith. Away from the white man, however, gathered in the slave quarters or down by the river in secret meetings, slaves often professed religion of a different kind. As an ex-slave explained, "When I starts preaching I couldn't read or write and had to preach what Master told me, and he say tell them niggers iffen they obeys the master they goes to Heaven; but I knowed they're something better for them but daren't tell them 'cept on the sly. That I done lots. I tells 'em iffen they keeps praying, the Lord will set 'em free."

While for some, resistance meant rebuking God, for others "resistance to tyrants was obedience to God." This latter group worshipped the God who delivered the Israelites, the God who meant black people to be free, the God who would bring divine retribution on the white oppressor. Anthony Burns, the object of a celebrated fugitive slave case, addressed himself to the issue: "You charge in escaping, I disobeyed God's law. No, indeed. That law which God wrote on the table of my heart, inspiring the love of freedom, and impelling me to seek it at every hazard. I obeyed, and by the good hand of my God upon me, I walked out of the house of bondage."

According to ex-slave Charles Ball, "The idea of a Revolution in the conditions of the whites and the blacks is the cornerstone of the religion of the latter." Sometimes slave preachers sought to convert this generalized conviction into a base for collective action of one kind or another. Religious meetings, as a white Virginian suspected, made fine "veils for revolutionary schemes." It was no accident, therefore, that a number of black rebels both led worship services and drew on Biblical teachings in plotting their insurrections, and that among them were Denmark Vesey of South Carolina and Nat Turner of Virginia.

SECTION 2. RUNAWAYS, RESISTERS, REVOLUTIONARIES

Many thousands of slaves chose to fight the system that bound them by running away, so many, in fact, that a regular feature of practically every issue of every Southern newspaper was the listing of runaway slave advertisements. However, only a small fraction of those who made the attempt were able to reach an area where they could be free. Although estimates of the number of fugitive slaves range as high as sixty thousand to one hundred thousand, the most recently published student of the problem, Larry Gara, who wisely does not commit himself to a specific estimate, believes the figure was substantially lower. One thing is certain, however: in the face of overwhelming odds, black men and women, sometimes with their children, persistently tried to escape.

How to keep "De Old Folks at Home" was perhaps the most time consuming and expensive of all the slaveholder's difficulties in managing his estate. Reluctant to acknowledge any imperfections in the system of slavery or in their own administration of it, many masters (sometimes with justification) blamed outsiders — abolitionists and free Negroes — for putting the idea of freedom in the minds of the slaves. Samuel Cartwright, a doctor of medicine at the University of Louisiana, came up with another diagnosis: runaways, he wrote quite seriously, suffered from "Draptomania, or the Disease Causing Negroes to Run Away."

Those who attempted escape were predominately, but by no means exclusively, the young, the energetic, the independent, and the intelligent. (Advertisements often described runaways as "talented and wily," "very intelligent," "uncommonly bright.") Flight, for at least some of the young, may have been stimulated by the identity crisis that, to a degree, affects all youth. For these slaves, running away represented a crucial rejection of "parental" authority, in their case the authority of the master. Vulnerable at once to hurt and hope, anxious to throw off the old and get on with the new, seeking to pledge their energies to a daring undertaking, these young slaves, it seems reasonable to suggest, were establishing their manhood as they made their break for freedom.

For all runaways, the principal motivation was the desire to be free, but any number of factors could trigger the flight. Consistent overwork and poor treatment, or perhaps a sudden change in conditions, such as impending sale or punishment, might be the catalytic circumstance. After a slave had committed a crime, or been charged with committing one, it was to be expected that he would try to escape. The family situation was a further consideration: the slave might leave to join a loved one or to get away from an unloved one; or he might run away in retaliation for the splitting up of his family by the owner. Then too, news that one more slave had gotten free or a camp meeting's rousing exhortation to freedom might embolden yet another to escape.

But there was much to deter potential fugitives. Strict surveillance, compounded with paternalism, weakened their resolve. Furthermore, the ignorant, superstitious, and fearful, naturally enough, preferred the devil they knew to the devil they might find outside. With scant experience of the world beyond the immediate plantation environs, most were in the position of the ex-slave who admitted he "had heard tell of a free country — but I did not know where it was, nor how to get there." Moreover, if flight were attempted, food and security would be difficult to find, and if flight were to fail, slaves well knew, punishment or sale into the deeper South almost certainly awaited. The pain of parting from family and friends restrained others. "It is my opinion," Douglass remarked, "that thousands would escape from slavery who now remain, but for the strong cords of affection that bind them to their friends."

Yet they did run away and, if caught, sometimes ran away again and even again. Possibly affecting disguises and traveling usually at night, the fugitives, who left singly or in an occasional group of as many as fifty, headed in all directions away from the plantation. The fortunate ones escaped to Canada, to Mexico, to Spanish Louisiana, and to Florida. (In Florida they allied with the Seminoles and fought two wars, the first in 1812–1818 and the second in 1835–1842, against the United States.) During the American Revolution and the War of 1812, thousands fled behind British lines.

If they were unable to get to free territory, runaways might hole up in the mountains, forests, or swamps. In these rough regions, some formed temporary and even permanent settlements. Frederick Law Olmsted, the perspicacious Northern newspaperman come South, was told by Southerners of Negroes who were born and bred, and who died, in such outposts. The Dismal Swamp in Virginia and North Carolina was a natural six-hundred-square-mile refuge. Virginia records tell of a deputy sheriff dispatched to bring back an escaped bondsman, who found his quarry plunged neck deep in swampy mire. Not foolhardy enough to go in after the fugitive, the deputy returned to his station and wrote on the warrant, "See-able but not come at-able."

The commitment to run away had a hard finality about it. As one slave explained, "if they undertake to escape, it is with a feeling of victory or death — they determine not to be taken alive, if possible to prevent it even by bloodshed." There were stories about slaves like Margaret Garner who, when she discovered the Negro catchers hot on her heels, tried to kill all her children and did succeed in stabbing one to death.

The philosophy undergirding the commitment was perhaps most succinctly expressed by William Wells Brown who, in his slave narrative, observed: "If I wish to stand up and say, 'I am a man,' I must leave the land that gave me birth."

One of the most subtle forms of retaliation against the master was the affecting of the role of Sambo, or Uncle Tom. Ironically enough it was the slaveowner himself who, to some degree, invented the role. Slaves, he averred many times, were naturally lazy, irresponsible, fawning, childlike, docile, and helpless. For if white Southerners could convince themselves and others that blacks were really inferior, they could justify maintaining slavery. But Sambo was far more the creation of the black Southerner. Moreover, it was a deliberate creation, even though, as Stanley Elkins, in a brilliantly controlled statement (Slavery), has pointed out, the absolute power of the Southern enslaver over the enslaved doubtless did cause some slaves to become permanently infantilized. An impressive body of social-psychological research reveals that some persons, slaves or no, can play a role with such intensity that, over a period of time, the role and the personality become indistinguishable. Most slaves, however, willfully fell to playing the Sambo role for reasons of survival and resistance. "The only weapon of self-defense that I could use successfully," noted ex-slave Henry Bibb, "was that of deception." Behind the mask, the slave could hide a simple desire to get out of work or gain a reward, along with his enjoyment at the luxury of having put something over on the master. Or Sambo could be masking an emotion so complex he did not really comprehend it: for example, his need to ease guilt feelings over his abiding hatred of his master.

Stupidity, incompetence, slowness were all components of the disguise. Douglass commented that "slaveholders ever underrate the intelligence with which they have to grapple," noting that among his co-laborers, a popular proverb was: "Where ignorance is bliss, 'tis folly to be wise." Was it ignorance or deception when slave mothers fell asleep over their sick children, thus forcing the white mistress to remain up through the night to care for them? Was it ignorance or deception when slaves refused to take up a trade? Was it ignorance or deception when blacks worked so poorly that numbers of whites had to be present to direct and help them?

A number of "first-rate tricks to dodge work," as an ex-slave put it, were devised by blacks. They demonstrated such a lack of finesse in maneuvering a plow that this cumbersome and tiring instrument had to be abandoned, and such was also the case with other work tools. A colonial traveler reported that the Negro seemed unable to adapt himself satisfactorily to either the hoe or the wheelbarrow. "Let a hundred men show him how to hoe, or drive a wheelbarrow, he'll still take the one by the Bottom and the other by the Wheel; and they often die before they can be conquered." So many hoes were "accidentally" broken by slaves that a heavier, and therefore work-slowing, "nigger hoe" had to be substituted. Planters would have been surprised to learn that the hoe was one of the basic tools of West African agriculture.

Slaves slogged through their work days half-heartedly; consequently, their labor yielded less than could have been produced by free men. By insisting that certain tasks demanded more than one worker, slaves aided one another in reducing the work load. A naive Southern diarist, Susan Smedes, wrote despairingly that an entire afternoon was used up by two of the men to butcher a sheep. Sometimes blacks performed so inadequately that one of the white men on the plantation was forced, disgustedly, to finish off the work himself.

At times that seemed unbearable, slaves walked away from the plantation. Solomon Northup bore witness that slaves, "when sick, or so worn out as to be unable to perform their task, escape into the swamps, willing to suffer the punishment inflicted for such offenses, in order to obtain a day or two of rest." Occasionally, a number took off together, a "stampede" Southerners called it, and this could result in giving the escapees a bargaining position with the master. Favorably positioned in the woods, they might sound out the master through an intermediary (perhaps a slave from a neighboring plantation or one of their own band), as to the possibility of better conditions of work generally and, specifically, more frequent rewards. Sometimes these negotiations, if they got to that stage, were successful, and the slaves achieved a minor victory. Often they received only punishment.

That something like collective bargaining should, on occasion, take place between master and slave should not be surprising. As Fredrickson and Lasch have suggested in an article comparing slavery with the penal institution, a certain amount of give and take, a degree of corruption of authority, was a necessity for both systems to function without major disruption. Many slaves became extremely resourceful in matters of survival and, beyond that, in exploiting the system. They read the master, the overseer, the slave driver, anyone in a command position, and learned how far and in what ways these men could be manipulated. The opportunistic slave, he of the delicate probings and the sensitive shifts, stood a far better chance of remaining psychically alive than did the slave who gave in, identified himself with the system, and, in Douglass's words, thereby became "transformed into a brute."

Often in the guise of Sambo, resisting slaves relied on various kinds of sabotage to bring at least minor irritation and expense to their owners. Observations on this point from various sources follow.

A *Virginia slaveholder:* It always seems on the plantations as if they took pains to break all the tools and spoil all the cattle that they possibly can, even when they know they'll be directly punished for it.

American newspaperman and landscapist Frederick Law Olmsted: . . . There were, for instance, under my observation, gates left open and bars let down against standing orders; rails removed from fences by the negroes (as was conjectured, to kindle their fires with), mules lamed, and implements broken, by careless usage; a flat boat, carelessly secured, going adrift on the river. . . .

English visitor Charles Lyell: . . . Thoughtless negroes allowed the chimney of our steam boat to get so choked up with soot that we were forced to quit it and travel by land.

American editor James Redpath: Whenever we came to a hill, especially if it was very steep, he [the slave] dismounted, lashed the horses with all his strength, varying his performance by picking up stones, none of them smaller than half a brick, and throwing with all his force, at the horse's legs. He seldom missed.

Ex-slave John Holmes: One overseer we had . . . worked the people hard, night and day. . . . He wanted I should blow the horn [to call the slaves to work] but I wouldn't undertake it. . . . One time I found it, and threw it in the river. . . . The overseer threatened us with a hundred lashes, unless we would find it. [The overseer] got another horn. I don't believe he blew it three times before it was gone, — it was in the river. We got up afterward without a horn. Several times, horns were got for the farm, but they could not keep them.

Feigning illness was another method of resistance, one that an owner had especial difficulty in handling. Often he found it better to accept the slave's word than to accuse him of sham, and send him back to the fields, only to have him turn out to be really sick. Olmsted cited one such case, when a slave had died, the owner lamenting: "He was a good eight hundred dollar nigger, and it was a lesson to me about taming possums, that I ain't going to forget in a hurry." On the auction block, a slave might pretend to be sick so that he would not be sold or would bring a smaller price, in order to spite the master, or perhaps, so that his new owner might give him a lighter work load. Feigned pregnancies were not uncommon even though, at the end of nine months, punishment was certain. According to Susan Smedes, one slave faked blindness for years and was given few duties, but after being freed was able to harvest some eighteen crops. It is worthwhile to note that, in the few compilations of plantation records of slave sicknesses made to date, the sick rolls were the longest at those times of the year when the work load was heaviest. Furthermore, there was a high incidence of ailments on Saturday work days, and very few on Sunday rest days.

The agony of slavery pushed some black men and women to resist through desperate acts of self-violence. To avoid work or auction block, slaves chopped off fingers and toes. They plied themselves with herbs that induced vomiting and with drugs that induced miscarriage. Dirt-eating rendered others unfit for work and, eventually, killed them. In *The Peculiar Institution,* Kenneth Stampp cites such instances as that of the Arkansas slave who, whenever wearied by work, would throw his left shoulder out of place, and of another man who was kicked by a mule and continued to aggravate the bruise whenever it began to heal. The desperation extended to suicide and a peculiar form of mercy killing.

Ex-slave accounts tell of the woman who hurled herself out a window to escape the rape-minded slave catcher, and of the runaway who slit his throat on board the ship that was carrying him back to slavery, and of Elizabeth, who smothered her own child.

Slave resistance was manifested in other types of violence or crime — and as Jordan has asked how do you distinguish crime from resistance among slaves? — including theft, arson, maiming, as well as poisoning and other forms of murder. Petty thievery was common, taking in such necessaries as money, clothing, food and animals, as well as such comforts as whiskey, wine, and jewelry. After theft, the most pervasive crime was arson. Seeking revenge for a general or specific wrong, slaves fired homes of overseers and masters, farm buildings, cotton gins, and fields. In the 1790's some citizens of Charleston were sufficiently alarmed to try to persuade others to build with brick and stone rather than wood. So widespread was arson that for a time the American Fire Insurance Company refused to insure any property in the South.

Provoked to sudden rage or brooding over accumulated injustices, slaves were driven to strike out at the white man over them, sometimes to kill him. How badly the white man was injured might depend on what weapon was available to the slave, stick or rock, brick or hoe, rope or knife, hatchet or axe. One ex-slave revealed that on his plantation blacks were given to stringing a rope across the road to knock passing riders from their horses; and another told of an old slave who, having been bullwhipped by the overseer, struck him in the head with a stick and then took up an axe, and chopped off his hands and feet. Into the master's food or drink house servants covertly slipped such poisons as arsenic, laudanum, ratsbane, and the seed of the jimson weed. It was a form of revenge peculiarly suited to women. After hearing that her master had provided for her in his will in the event he left no heirs, one slave woman proceeded to poison his three children, one by one. Actually, not a few slaves did murder the overseer or master or mistress or even, occasionally, the whole family. In Virginia alone, records reveal that between 1786 and 1810 thirty-one slaves were executed for killing masters and overseers.

Most slaves had either witnessed or, more likely, heard some gory tale of murder. There was the old woman who, furious over a reprimand from the overseer, seized a hoe and chopped him to death. And there was Cicely in Mississippi who slew master, wife, and two children with the blows of a broad axe. Southern whites lived with an unremitting fear. "The night bell never tolled for fire in Richmond," John Randolph of Virginia wrote, "that the mother did not hug her infant more closely to her bosom."

Beyond day-by-day resistance, revolts erupted from time to time during the entire span of slavery, occurring as early as 1663 in Gloucester County, Virginia, and breaking out periodically thereafter in rural and urban areas of both North and South. Some were elaborately planned and organized and had as their intention the destruction of the slave system and the creation of a black state; others tended to be more haphazardly put together and aimed only at wiping out the slaveholder's life and property. Still others were concerned mainly with throwing off the bonds of servitude through flight.

Marion Kilson, relying heavily on Aptheker's work, has isolated several socio-economic factors which he believes have contributed to the outbreak of slave rebellions. These include the type of plantation system, ease of communication (closeness to city or transportation), abrupt population shifts (frequently resulting in a larger population of Negroes in a particular area), currency of revolutionary ideas in the culture, and forceful individual leadership. To these might be added the economic conditions, often harsh at times of revolution, and, in at least a few known cases, a strong religious thrust.

If one still asks, why did slaves revolt, then he must consider the creative–destructive impulses in man. The man who cannot or is not allowed to create, who has been prevented from developing his potential — as the slave was systematically and deliberately prevented from developing his — needs to destroy. If the destruction is performed in conjunction with others, that is, in a mass uprising or revolt, the sense of creating something while actually destroying may be heightened. It is not unreasonable to assume that the feelings of the slaves participating in a revolt were somewhat akin to the emotions of some of those taking part in the urban riots of the 1960's — and those persons experienced a strong sense of unity, shared pride, exhilaration, and even joy. An observer reported of the 1739 Stono, South Carolina, rebellion, that after slaves burned and killed along a twelve-mile swath, having found rum to drink on the way, they ran into an open field, "and began to sing and dance, by way of triumph."

Underlying all the other causes for revolt was the massive injustice that emanated from, indeed, was at the very core of the South's peculiar social system. As Hannah Arendt, and before her Herman Melville in *Billy Budd,* has pointed out, there are those fearful times when violence appears to be the only possibility for righting an awful wrong. This is not to say it is right. It is rather to note with sadness what one can expect from human beings when they are treated brutally by other human beings.

Of the numerous slave revolts, at least six reached serious stages and had appalling repercussions. In 1712 in New York City more than two dozen slaves fired a building and killed at least nine men, wounding several others. The city, chilled by the murders of a Long Island family only four years earlier, for which four slaves had been executed, reacted quickly and without mercy. Soldiers from a nearby fort rounded up most of the rebels in a matter of hours, although several evaded capture by taking their own lives. The remainder were executed: thirteen were hanged, one was suspended in chains in the town until death, three were burned, one being roasted over a slow fire, and one was broken on the wheel. Twenty-nine years later, against a backdrop of severe winter and economic suffering, with the added aggravation of several barn-burnings by Negroes across the river in Hackensack and the threat of a Spanish invasion, New York City again was enveloped in tragedy. A series of fires broke out at key governmental buildings, and the rumor spread quickly that Negroes had been seen in the area. Whether an actual slave conspiracy existed can never be known; but, in any event, the facts made little difference to a community engulfed in hysteria. Well over a hundred and fifty persons, including some whites who were thought to be accomplices, were rounded up; thirty-one slaves were finally executed, another seventy were driven out of the colony.

The most serious revolt of the colonial period, in which more than twenty white persons were killed, erupted in Stono, South Carolina, southwest of Charleston, in 1739. Previous months had seen hard economic conditions, slave guerrilla warfare, and rumors of a conspiracy which had led to the arrest of three slaves. In addition, South Carolina's population was heavily imbalanced, black over white. One September day a group of slaves met at Stono, where they killed the guards at a warehouse and stocked up on arms and ammunition, and then marched out into the countryside "with colours flying and drums beating." Heading to the southwest, toward Spanish territory where they could find refuge, they killed the whites and burned the plantations on their route, picking up more slaves as they went, until their number reached an estimated fifty to one hundred. When they stopped to rest and celebrate, the militia caught up with them and surrounded the field, and, in the encounter that followed a number were killed. In the next months, others were captured and put to death.

In the hot late summer of 1800, a young giant of a man named

Gabriel Prosser, but called "General" by his fellow slaves, conspired to gain control of Richmond, and perhaps the whole state of Virginia, to set up a black commonwealth. Reputed to possess an "intellect above his rank in life," Gabriel derived his inspiration from "divine signals" and an exposure to the French revolutionary philosophy. For some weeks before the target date, he matured his plans, organizing a cadre, pinpointing strategic installations in the city, and accumulating a small cache of weapons. During the same period he enlisted an indeterminate but decidedly substantial number of recruits, later reckoned by frightened witnesses at from two thousand to fifty thousand. On the appointed day, Gabriel and his men gathered outside the city. But nature — the impartial nature of the weather, which rains on the powerful and the rebellious alike, and the capricious nature of man, with his tragically divided loyalties — aborted the insurrection. A storm, bringing "enormous rain," hindered the movements of Gabriel's forces, washing out a key bridge and making normally quiet streams impassable, even as two slaves were informing on their fellows. Retaliation ensued, so bloody that Thomas Jefferson was provoked to remark, "We are truly to be pitied."

In the same year Gabriel lost his bid to escape slavery, Denmark Vesey won a $1,500 lottery and purchased his freedom. Prior to his good fortune, Vesey had been the long-time personal servant of Captain Joseph Vesey, a slave trader, and so had travelled widely, gaining facility in several languages. Once freed, Vesey set up a carpentry shop in Charleston, South Carolina. Over the next years he acquired money and property, and built a reputation for industry and integrity among both whites and blacks. Living free, however, he had a vantage point from which to evaluate the debasement of all black men, regardless of their legal status, as well as an unusual opportunity to take independent action. He began to jibe at the slaves and free Negroes who hung around his shop over their passivity and subservience to the white man. Moreover, he joined the African Methodist Episcopal Church, later becoming a preacher, where he argued that God's intention was for black people to be free. Stressing the parallels between the children of Israel and the slaves of the South, Vesey told his congregations of the work of the abolitionists and held up the example of the Haitians' winning their own independence.*

---

*In 1804 Haitian blacks, under the leadership of Toussaint L'Ouverture, defeated a French army and took control of the island – freeing all slaves and killing or chasing away the whites; the revolt took ten years to succeed.

Around Christmas of 1821, when he felt his arguments had been properly received and disseminated, Vesey began to build a secret organization geared to rebellion. In the next months he showed himself to be both a dedicated revolutionary and a skilled psychologist. Only the most intelligent and capable slaves, along with the leaders of the A.M.E. church, were enlisted, and they were warned that once a commitment had been made, they could not retreat. Furthermore, his closest lieutenants were selected for their peculiar qualities and positions, granted them because of their owners' trust. Rolla, servant of the governor of South Carolina, a position with obvious advantages for the plotters, was described as "bold" and "ardent," with "uncommon self-possession." The ship carpenter Peter Poyas, as foresighted as he was determined, has been quoted as warning: "Don't mention it to those waiting-men who receive presents of old coats from their masters, or they'll betray us." Gullah Jack, master of witchcraft, was brought in to give his supernatural blessing to the conspirators, some of whom were true believers. Along the line of occult persuasion, Vesey himself might well have played up his own epilepsy to sway the superstitious.

Only the small group of leaders was aware of the plan that called for a six-pronged attack on Charleston on Sunday, July 16, 1822. Orders were to seize all arms and ammunition and to cut down all whites. Further, Vesey informed his followers that help could probably be expected from the Haitians, whom he had written, and that their ships might await at the docks to take the rebels to Haiti. As an added stimulus to revolt, the conspirators spread rumors that whites intended to massacre blacks on the Fourth of July. In fact, something like that did happen. It was too optimistic to expect that Vesey's terrible secret could be kept for so long. In late May an unauthorized recruiter attempted to sign up a "faithful" house slave. Ultimately forty-two men were banished, thirty-five executed.

Again in 1800, the year when Gabriel died and Denmark Vesey bought his way out of slavery, Nat Turner was born in Southampton County, Virginia. His African mother, it is reported, was so upset at giving birth to a child who would be a slave that she had to be restrained from killing him. As is the case for most slave revolutionaries, little is known of Nat's life, but from the rather skimpy record it appears that he was an exceptional slave. His family life seems to have been notably strong; according to his own testimony, he was taught by his parents to read and write. At one time in his life he ran away, only to return later because he believed he had been divinely instructed to do so.

Through years of Bible reading and intermittent visions, Nat became convinced that God intended him "for some great purpose." His mysticism not only provided inspiration but also attracted followers. "Having soon discovered that to be great I must appear so," he explained, "I studiously avoided mixing in society and wrapped myself in mystery, devoting my time to fasting and prayer."

On August 21, 1831, after he had fully prepared himself, and having read the proper signs in the heavens, Nat called his followers together to map final plans. That night he and five other slaves set out, armed with axes and clubs, gathering forces as they moved from plantation to plantation. Turner later declared, "indiscriminate slaughter was not their intention after they obtained a foothold, and was resorted to in the first instance to strike terror and alarm. Women and children would afterwards have been spared, and men too who ceased to resist." Whatever his intention, some fifty-five white persons were killed before a combined force of the army, the militia, and numerous white volunteers — some three thousand men in all — could put down the rebellion. The white forces did not stop with Turner's band, but went on to slaughter blacks at random throughout the area; the dead finally numbered nearly two hundred.

Harriet Jacobs, an ex–Virginia slave, later reflected sardonically: "Not far from this time Nat Turner's insurrection broke out; and the news threw our town into great commotion. Strange that they should be alarmed, when their slaves were so contented and happy."

SECTION 3. RESISTANCE IN THE NORTH

On the eve of the Civil War some two hundred and fifty thousand blacks, classified as free Negroes but often calling themselves the "half-free," resided in the North. A complex of local, state, and federal legislation, as well as custom based on prejudice (what fugitive Samuel Ringgold Ward called "the ever-present, ever-crushing Negro-hate"), severely limited their possibilities. Residence was denied them in a number of states, while nearly everywhere they were barred legally from exercising political rights. It was the rare Negro man or woman who was not locked into essentially menial employment, such as white-washer, drayman, huckster, riverman, cook, or washerwoman. Ghettos were already a part of the urban North and segregation (not by law but mostly by practice) extended into practically every area and institution. "We don't allow niggers in here," Frederick Douglass acidly noted, was a predictable Northern white welcome. Everywhere blacks were the subject of ridicule and contempt, white parents admonishing their children to behave, or else "that old nigger will carry you off." A Negro civil rights advocate, John I. Gaines of Cleveland, sadly observed: "no place of distinction is held out to the black man, no path of glory opened to his vision; he may thrive if he can, is at liberty to die, but is nowhere encouraged, fostered or protected."

Unwilling to tolerate the situation as it existed for their people, black leaders employed every constitutional means at hand to pursue their twin goals—equal rights for Negroes and the abolition of slavery. To these ends, they came together in protest meetings of various sorts and held state and national conventions, besides editing and publishing seventeen different newspapers. Moreover, they authored addresses which were then circulated among the blacks and whites, petitioned the various governmental bodies, and sent out lecturers across the North, always trying to point out the inconsistencies and hypocrisies in American life so that people might see the need to reform. Along with an occasional attempt at legal amendment, these protest activities, often undertaken in alliance with whites, constituted the major effort of the Northern black leadership.

However, discrimination, segregation, and slavery were also challenged by black Northerners through both individual and collective acts of resistance. When, for instance, Robert Purvis's children were repeatedly turned away from the public schools of Philadelphia, he reacted by refusing to pay his 1853 school tax. In San Francisco as well, two Negro merchants, protesting their disfranchisement in 1857, withheld payment of their poll taxes. This idea was extended by a prominent abolitionist, Charles Lenox Remond, the very model of defiance, who proposed, "Let every colored man, called upon to pay taxes to any institution in which he is deprived or denied its privileges and advantages, withhold his taxes, though it costs imprisonment or confiscation. Let our motto be — No privileges, no pay."

Segregated accommodations in public houses and churches, and on public conveyances, presenting as they did a direct insult to the individual, provoked black resistance. Addressing himself to the separate seating arrangements in the churches, Frederick Douglass urged communicants to sit where they chose and to passively resist while ministers and the church elders dragged them out. A Negro in a Massachusetts small town won a court case to keep his pew in the local Baptist Church, but the white parishioners subjected him to so much harassment, including tarring and feathering his pew and removing his chair, that he finally surrendered and left.

Incidents of black men sitting in railroad cars reserved for whites, only to be forcibly removed, were reported periodically in newspapers during the two decades before the war. Douglass, whose whole life exemplified resistance, stubbornly insisted upon nondiscriminatory railroad accommodations, therefore clashing on a number of occasions with railroad employees. When the conductor would ask him to retire to the car for colored persons, he would reply, "If you will give me any good reason why I should leave this car, I'll go willingly, but without such reason, I do not feel at liberty to leave." A scuffle inevitably followed, as railroad employees pulled Douglass toward the Jim Crow section, the black resister grimly dragging behind several seats he had uprooted from their moorings.

The most ambitious form of resistance by Northern Negroes was the underground railroad. Recent scholarship has shown it to be both less organized and less dominated by whites than formerly romance had depicted. In actuality, the slave who determined to run away was in large part left to his own resources. Help was minimal or nonexistent until he reached the North. Once there, if he were not left to fend for himself, as frequently happened, he most often was cared for by free Negroes because, on the one hand, the authorities and those who made it their business to look out for runaways were likely to be suspicious of a black among whites, and on the other hand, the fugitive himself, understandably, was likely to believe white benefactors somewhat less trustworthy than black.

A handful of blacks made periodic trips into the South to lead slaves to freedom. Among the valiant number was the free Negro Leonard Grimes, a fairly prosperous hack driver in Washington, D. C., who acted as a conductor of escaping slaves until he was caught and sent to prison. On his release, he went to Boston where he became a Baptist preacher and continued to give succor to runaways. Best-known of the conductors was the legendary Harriet Tubman. An escaped slave herself, Harriet Tubman made a number of slave-stealing visits to the South, nineteen by some counts, proving so successful that a $40,000 reward was offered for her capture. If any of her party became timorous and wanted to go back, her biographer reported, Harriet would cock her pistol and volunteer, "Dead Niggers tell no tales. You go or die." Whether true or no, the story is indicative of both the courage of the woman and the danger of the operation.

If the slave managed to reach the North, and his chances for recapture far outweighed those for success, he generally could rely on assistance from Negro middlemen, many of whom exploited their occupations for the cause. Boatmen stowed away fugitives on vessels bound farther North or rowed them across the Ohio river, the demarcation line between slavery and freedom, in skiffs. In like manner, workers on trains hid slaves behind luggage and boxes in baggage cars. In most Northern cities one or two Negroes had the reputation of providing runaways with warm accommodations and sound advice. In New York City the welcome-light burned at the homes of the clergymen Charles B. Ray and Henry Highland Garnet. If stopping at Syracuse, slaves stayed with the Reverend Jermain Wesley Loguen, at Buffalo, with abolitionist-writer William Wells Brown, at Boston, with former slave Lewis Hayden, and at Newport, with the caterer George T. Downing. Lawyer John Mercer Langston willingly compromised his position as township clerk of Oberlin, during the latter part of the 1850's, to provide food and lodging for fugitives.

Organized efforts to aid runaways, the vigilance committees which surfaced as early as the mid-1830's, were operated either wholly or in the main by Negroes, numbering among their leaders those persons just mentioned. Although supported largely through penny-nickel-dime contributions. the vigilance committees were able to perform countless services. In addition to food, clothing and shelter, they furnished legal aid, forged freedom papers, found jobs, and, in general, comforted the fugitive in his stressful situation. Two of the most energetic organizations were the New York Committee of Vigilance, headed by the indefatigable David Ruggles, and the General Vigilance Committee of Philadelphia, of which the most active member was William Still, the author of a mammoth volume highly useful to scholars even though increasingly suspect, on the underground railroad. In northeastern Ohio, fertile ground for abolitionists where a number of committees accordingly operated, black abolitionists expressed defiance of the slavery powers openly. Prominently displayed in an 1852 parade at the opening of the state Negro convention in Cleveland was a vigilance committee banner, depicting Hercules with a club, the master slavery at his feet, and, beyond, a black woman with chains broken.

Thousand of slaves, fearing a return to slavery and finding less than liberty in the North, carried their resistance a step further by continuing on to Canada. Many free Negroes, discouraged by the overwhelming difficulty of life in the North, joined them, sometimes with a shove in that direction from whites — as in the case of the mass migration from Cincinnati in 1829, when, after an assault by white mobs on the Negro section, more than half the black population fled.

By the 1850's the emigration issue was widely discussed and debated. Some black leaders believed that to leave the country would at once strengthen the slavery institution, by removing the influence and example of free Negroes, and deny the Negro's right to the enjoyment of the country's fruits, earned, they felt, by long labor on its soil. Indeed, many had long opposed the white-dominated American Colonization Society on those very grounds. Others saw emigration as a means of resistance. One-time Harvard student Martin R. Delany, who emphasized the benefits of a fierce pride in African roots, explained, "I shall never be reconciled to live among them [whites], subservient to their will." The Reverend Henry Highland Garnet, leader of the African Civilization Society, also endorsed the idea of emigration as a way of obtaining status as a full-fledged citizen of a nation, with the freedom and privileges necessary to achieve manhood. These ideas were articulated by twenty-one-year-old John Mercer Langston at the 1849 Ohio state convention. Although he "dearly" loved his native land, he began, it offered him no protection, and therefore he was willing to go wherever he could be free. So long as strong prejudice existed, and he saw "little hope for its removal," it was impossible for Negroes to have a nationality as Americans, and yet a nationality was necessary "before we can become anybody." Blacks must therefore leave the country; to remain would be humiliating, "virtually acknowledging our inferiority to the white man." A few years later Langston himself changed his mind, but others were not only advocating but participating in emigration schemes. Besides Canada, suggested destinations were Kansas, lower California, the Far West, the Carribean, Australia, the Pacific Islands, and Africa. Emigration conventions were held in 1854, 1856, and 1858 to stir interest and draw up proposals, but serious discussion ended with the start of the Civil War.

Other black Northerners, from time to time, through state and national conventions, explored the possibilities of abandoning the cities for the less inhibiting countryside, where they might set up schools, churches, and machinery and, as one state convention, in the purest American vein, optimistically declared, "live, work and be happy." Several black communities actually were established, but for most free Negroes, the absence of funds, and the powerful difficulties of simply sustaining daily existence dictated that the utopian dream remain only that.

By choice or not, most Northern blacks were confronted with life as it was in the United States. Remarkably, a considerable number were able not only to survive and continue to protest their status and the condition of their brothers in the South, but also to achieve secure and respected places in society. The Reverend Samuel Ringgold Ward, one of a number of ex-slaves who rendered important service as an antislavery orator, explained in his autobiography that he considered any activity that cultivated "the upward tendencies of the coloured man" to be an antislavery activity. "I call the expert black cordwainer, blacksmith, or other mechanic or artisan, the teacher, the lawyer, the doctor, the farmer, or the divine, an anti-slavery labourer"; he wrote, "and in his vocation from day to day, with his hoe, hammer, pen, tongue, or lancet, he is living down the base calumnies of his heartless adversaries — he is demonstrating his truth and their falsity."

Besides the nameless throng who, as Ward suggests, insisted on decent and honorable lives, however modest, and thereby rebuffed the forces that pressed indecency and dishonor upon them, there were others who by the same token accomplished conspicuously in professions ranging from business to poetry. These included Paul Cuffe, Massachusetts shipowner, and James Forten, wealthy sail-manufacturer in Philadelphia, as well as mathematician-astronomer Benjamin Banneker who helped to lay out Washington, D. C. Among the ministers were Daniel A. Payne and J. W. C. Pennington; among the lawyers, Robert Morris, Jr., and Macon B. Allen; among the teachers, Charles L. Reason and William H. Allen — the first, professor of mathematics and *belles lettres* and the second, professor of languages, at Centre College in McGrawville, New York. Among the doctors were James McCune Smith and James McCrummell; the journalists included John B. Russworm, the first black graduate of a college in this country (Bowdoin College, 1826) and co-editor with Samuel Cornish of the first black newspaper, *Freedom's Journal* (1827). In the arts there were the singer Eliza Greenfield, "the Black Swan," and the poets James Whitfield and Francis Ellen Watkins.

After the passage in 1850 of the Fugitive Slave Act, which forbade the alleged runaway both the right to testify and the right to a trial by jury and also assumed his guilt rather than his innocence, Negroes stepped up their resistance. Across the North meetings were held to denounce the law, which a black Ohio convention deemed "first on the catalogue of disgraceful and abominable legislation." A Negro convention in Casenovia, New York, called on all slaves to run away and, at the same time, to be prepared to kill anyone who might pursue them. In New York City, the black leadership, with a taste for irony, offered their allegiance to the motto of Virginia: "Resistance to tyranny is obedience to God." At an assembly in Westchester, noted abolitionist Robert Purvis vowed, "should any wretch enter my dwelling, any pale faced spectre among ye, to execute this law on me or mine, I'll seek his life, I'll shed his blood." Elsewhere, individuals and groups alike championed resistance by varied means.

Direct action followed talk. Forty-two Negroes in Chicago formed the Liberty Association, pledging themselves to keep close watch out for possible slave-catchers, and blacks in other localities did the same. In the southern Pennsylvania town of Christiana, William Parker and his neighbors set up an "organization for mutual protection against slaveholders and kidnappers." In September of 1851 Edward Gorsuch and his party from nearby Maryland came into Christiana in search of his four runaway slaves, who had taken sanctuary in the Parker home. Gorsuch demanded entrance into the house, but at this moment Parker's wife let out a blast on a horn which brought Negro supporters to the scene. In the exchange of gunfire that followed, Gorsuch died and his son was wounded. A civilian posse aided by United States marines subsequently rounded up thirty-eight of the defenders, including three whites, but Parker and the slaves managed to elude them and arrived safely in Canada. In city after city sympathy meetings were held to celebrate what a Columbus, Ohio, group called the "victorious heroes at the battle of Christiana," and to collect contributions for the legal defense of the "Christiana sufferers."

Slave rescues had long been a part of the black resistance movement in the North, but the Fugitive Slave Law now gave them wider publicity and stronger white support than they had previously attracted. Throughout the fifties the Northern public thrilled, as Southern citizens glowered, over blow by blow accounts in the newspapers of the Shadrach, Thomas Sims, Anthony Burns, Jerry, and Oberlin–Wellington rescue cases, to name five of the most prominent. These incidents, and the attention paid them, had immeasurable influence on many wavering Northern consciences.

The Oberlin–Wellington rescue, occurring in September of 1858, may be taken as representative of the passion and commitment with which some Northern black and white citizens reacted to the Fugitive

Slave Law. A runaway named John Price, who had been sheltered for some months by the antislavery-dominated community of Oberlin, Ohio, was deliberately lured into a trap and seized by authorities, who hurried him to nearby Wellington where they awaited a train going south. However, word of the capture spread quickly through Oberlin, and at least fifty townspeople and Oberlin College students flooded into Wellington. They wrested Price from the authorities, then sped him to Canada and freedom.

Thirty-seven men, including twelve Negroes, were indicted. While the case was in the courts, black abolitionist John Langston, whose brother Charles was on trial for his part in the rescue, took to the public forum. He assured audiences that whenever the opportunity for rescue arose, Negroes would imitate the "worthy example" of the Oberlin–Wellington group; furthermore, he urged them to reinstate the Declaration of Independence and the Constitution, the former struck down by slavery and the latter by the Fugitive Slave Law. Discharging this obligation would involve sacrifice, he said, perhaps going to prison or marching to the battlefield — and if it were to battle, he predicted blacks and whites would march together. He longed himself to take the field, he declared, as "common soldier or in a more exalted rank," and "strike" for his country. Finally, a combination of protest and pressure, aroused by speeches such as Langston's and newspaper coverage, forced the authorities to drop the cases against all but two of the rescuers, who were fined and given short jail sentences.

As the frustrations and oppressions of past years coincided in the fifties with the worsening economic conditions for Negroes, the highly emotional atmosphere, and the overall refusal of the North to temper its "most cruel and bitter prejudice," the expressed willingness to resort to physical force was heard more frequently and from a larger segment of the black leadership. With the political and religious institutions in the country becoming increasingly more rigid and unresponsive to their problems, blacks began to suggest other, more disruptive alternatives. The Reverend Samuel Ringgold Ward was specific on the matter: "Such crises as these leave us the right of Revolution, and if need be, that right we will, at whatever cost, most sacredly maintain."

Not that the threat of violence had ever been absent. The call for black liberation had been sounded not only by Gabriel, Vesey, and Turner in the South in years past. Many black Northerners were well acquainted with, indeed had long debated the merits of the arguments for freedom-by-violence put forth by David Walker and the Reverend Henry Highland Garnet.

In 1829 Walker, a black Boston clothing dealer, published a seventy-six-page pamphlet, which came to be known as *Walker's Appeal*. Declaring that the Negroes of the United States were the "most wretched, degraded and abject set of beings that ever lived," Walker called upon slaves to undertake armed rebellion if their masters refused voluntarily to free them. Some fourteen years later at the black national convention at Buffalo, New York, a twenty-seven year old firebrand, Henry Highland Garnet, minister of an all-white Presbyterian congregation at Troy, New York, advocated similar sentiments in his "An Address to the Slaves of the United States." In the call-to-arms section, Garnet charged his fellow black men to arise. "Strike for your lives and liberties . . . . Rather die freemen than live to be slaves. Remember that you are Four Millions. Let your motto be resistance! *resistance!* RESISTANCE!" The adoption of the "Address" as the sentiment of the convention failed by only one vote.

Moreover, by the end of the forties an Ohio black convention was recommending that five hundred copies of *Walker's Appeal* and Garnet's "Address" be acquired and distributed throughout the state. The same year a black New York newspaper editor summoned the enslaved to strike for their freedom, writing, "Make up your minds to die rather than bequeath a state of slavery to your posterity."

As was true for practically any movement pertaining to black liberation, Frederick Douglass was in the vanguard of those calling for forcible resistance. Before a large crowd at Faneuil Hall in Boston in 1849, Douglass acknowledged that he would welcome word tomorrow, if it should come, that the slaves had risen up against their masters. Following the passage of the Fugitive Slave Act, he reflected that the only way to make that legislation "a dead letter" was to "make half a dozen or more dead kidnappers. The man who takes the office of a bloodhound ought to be treated as a bloodhound."

By the middle fifties Douglass was writing and talking of the need for black people to arm themselves. "Every colored man in the country," he advised, "should keep his revolver under his head, loaded and ready for use." Weapons should be given to runaways, and they should be instructed to defend themselves against anyone who might try to deprive them of their liberty. "This reproach must be wiped out," he insisted, "and nothing short of resistance on the part of the colored men, can wipe it out. Every slave hunter who meets a bloody death in his infernal business, is an argument in favor of the manhood of our race. Resistance is, therefore, wise as well as just."

Among other men and in many states the reactions were similar. The Reverend Garnet carried a gun with him wherever he went, while the Reverend Ward announced publicly he would "never be taken alive." Boston physician John Rock believed the time had come for blacks to demonstrate their manhood by some daring or desperate act. Their readiness to "protect our right to freedom at whatever cost" was affirmed by a group assembled at Portland, Maine. New York City blacks at a Presbyterian church in 1851, noting the importance of self-defense throughout history, agreed on the need for defensive weapons. Across the country in California in 1856, one of the delegates to a Negro state convention declared he would welcome a foreign invasion, if it would mean freedom for all black people. Following the Dred Scott decision,* which was universally denounced at black protest meetings, a fiery Charles Lenox Remond, his nonresistant period as a Garrisonian long since past, recommended to a New Bedford, Massachusetts, gathering that an address be prepared calling on slaves to overthrow their masters. And so it went.

Nowhere in the country was the tone more militant than among the black leadership of Ohio. As early as 1849 when they reinvigorated their convention movement, the higher-law philosophy had guided their attitudes and actions. Resolutions passed that year included a refusal to recognize any law that curtailed man's natural rights; a plea for slaves to run away and for northern freedmen to assist them in their flight; and a recommendation to circulate five hundred copies of the Walker-Garnet pamphlets, lately printed back to back. Two years later schoolteacher and dentist Charles Langston addressed the delegates, urging every slave "from Maryland to Texas, to arise and assist their liberties, and cut their masters' throats if they attempt again to reduce them to slavery."

In line with a similar evolution in aggressiveness among blacks across the country, a ten-man committee of Ohioans, in an 1856 resolution to the state legislature, warned: "If we are deprived of education, of equal political privileges, still subjected to the same depressing influences under which we now suffer, the natural consequences will follow, and the state, for her planting of injustice, will reap her harvest of sorrow and crime. She will contain within her limits a discontented population . . . dissatisfied, estranged . . . ready to welcome any revolution or invasion as a relief, for they can lose nothing and gain much."

Black military companies had been organized in Cleveland and Cincinnati earlier in the decade, and in 1857 convention delegates

---

* The Supreme Court decision in the Dred Scott case (1857) was based on the ruling that no Negro could claim the rights of a citizen, and that Congress had no power to deprive citizens of their slave-property without "due process of law."

resolved "where practicable" to set up other such groups to study Scott's military tactics and "to become more proficient in the use of arms." On the eve of Civil War, the position of Negro Ohio, certainly of its political spokesmen, and of a considerable body of black men in the North, was reflected in an Ohio state convention resolution. It hailed John Brown and his men, five of whom were Negroes, as the "Heralds and Prophets of that new lesson, the lesson of Insurrection."

More than a generation ago the Negro scholar Charles S. Johnson could lament the fact that Denmark Vesey was "a symbol of a spirit too violent to be acceptable to the whole community. There are no Negro schools named for him, and it would be extremely poor taste and bad judgment for the Negroes to take any pride in his courage and philosophy. There is, indeed, little chance for Negro youth to know about him at all."

In our generation some things have changed. Now a revolution is taking shape in the minds and hearts of black Americans. "Say it loud," says soul singer James Brown, "I'm black and I'm proud," and an ever expanding number of the young and old alike brandish their clutched fists into the air defiantly, as a symbol of resistance and liberation.†

Today David Walker and Frederick Douglass and Nat Turner live, in the way that other American spokesmen for freedom live. They are justly celebrated by many Americans, regardless of their color, as men who refused to accept less than the human rights that moral civilized men have always insisted are the inalienable birthright of us all.

SECTION 4.   A SELECTED BIBLIOGRAPHY

Addington, W. G. "Slave Insurrections in Texas," *Journal of Negro History* (1950).

*Aptheker, Herbert, ed. *A Documentary History of the Negro People in the United States*, I (1965).

*———. *American Negro Slave Revolts* (1952).

---

† Modern black militancy is the focus of a paperback Glencoe Press anthology of documents and analyses, *Black Power: the Radical Response to White America* (Insight Series, 1969) by Thomas Wagstaff.

* Available in paperback.

*———. Nat Turner's Slave Rebellion (1966).

*———. One Continual Cry — David Walker's Appeal, Its Setting, Its Meaning (1965).

*Austin Steward: Twenty-two Years a Slave and Forty Years a Freeman, with an introduction by Jane H. and William H. Pease (1969).

Bauer, Raymond A. and Bauer, Alice H. "Day to Day Resistance to Slavery," Journal of Negro History (1942).

Bell, Howard H. "Expressions of Negro Militancy in the North, 1840–1860," Journal of Negro History (1960).

———. "Negro Nationalism: A Factor in Emigration Projects, 1858–1861," Journal of Negro History (1962).

*Bennett, Lerone. Before the Mayflower (1962).

Bibb, Henry. Narrative of the Life and Adventures of Henry Bibb, An American Slave (1849).

*Botkin, B. A., ed. Lay My Burden Down (1945).

Brown, Sterling; Davis, Arthur; and Lee, Ulysses, eds. The Negro Caravan (1941).

Brown, William Wells. The Black Man (1863).

*———. Narrative of William Wells Brown, A Fugitive Slave, with an introduction by Larry Gara (1969).

*Clarke, John Henrik, ed. William Styron's Nat Turner — Ten Black Writers Respond (1968).

Clarke, T. W. "Negro Plot, 1741," New York History (1944).

*Davis, David Brion. "Slavery," in C. Vann Woodward, ed. The Comparative Approach to American History (1968).

*———. The Problem of Slavery in Western Culture (1966).

*Douglass, Frederick. Life and Times of Frederick Douglass (1882).

———. My Bondage and My Freedom (1855).

*Drew, Benjamin. The Refugee: A North-Side View of Slavery, with an introduction by Tilden G. Edelstein (1969).

Eakin, Sue and Logsdon, Joseph, eds. Solomon Northup, Twelve Years a Slave (1959).

*Elkins, Stanley M. Slavery (1959).

*Fisher, Miles Mark. Negro Slave Songs in the United States (1953).

Fredrickson, George M. and Lasch, Christopher. "Resistance to Slavery," Civil War History (1967).

*Gara, Larry. The Liberty Line (1961).

Genovese, Eugene D. "Rebelliousness and Docility in the Negro Slave:

---

* Available in paperback.

A Critique of the Elkins Thesis," *Civil War History* (1967).

———. "The Legacy of Slavery and the Roots of Black Nationalism," *Studies on the Left* (1966).

*Greene, Lorenzo Johnston. *The Negro in Colonial New England* (1942).

Halasz, Nicholas. *The Rattling Chains* (1966).

*Harding, Vincent. "Religion and Resistance among Antebellum Negroes, 1800–1860," in August Meier and Elliott Rudwick, eds., *The Making of Black America,* I (1960).

*Henson, Josiah. *An Autobiography of the Reverend Josiah Henson,* with an introduction by Robin W. Winks (1969).

Higginson, Thomas Wentworth. *Travellers and Outlaws* (1889).

Hughes, Langston and Bontemps, Arna, eds. *The Book of Negro Folklore* (1959).

*Jordan, Winthrop. *White Over Black* (1968).

Kilson, Marion D. de B. "Towards Freedom: An Analysis of Slave Revolts in the United States," *Phylon* (1964).

*Litwack, Leon. *North of Slavery* (1961).

Lofton, John. *Insurrection in South Carolina* (1964).

*Mannix, Daniel with Malcolm Cowley. *Black Cargoes* (1962).

McKibben, D. B. "Negro Slave Insurrections in Mississippi," *Journal of Negro History* (1949).

Miles, Edwin A. "The Mississippi Slave Insurrection Scare of 1835," *Journal of Negro History* (1957).

Mullin, Gerald. *Slave Resistance in Eighteenth Century Virginia* (Ph.D. dissertation, University of California, Berkeley, 1967).

*Nichols, Charles H. *Many Thousand Gone* (1963).

*Olmsted, Frederick Law. *A Journey in the Seaboard States* (1856).

*Pettigrew, Thomas. *Profile of the Negro American* (1964).

*Phillips, Ulrich B. *American Negro Slavery* (1966).

Porter, Kenneth. "Negroes and the Seminole War, 1835–1842," *Journal of Southern History* (1964).

Quarles, Benjamin. *Black Abolitionists* (1969).

*———, ed. *Narrative of the Life of Frederick Douglass* (1960).

"The Question of Sambo," Report of the Ninth Newberry Library Bulletin (1968).

Rawick, George. "The Historical Roots of Black Liberation," *Radical America* (1968).

*Redding, J. Saunders. *They Came in Chains* (1950).

---

* Available in paperback.

Russell, Marion J. "American Slave Discontent in Records of the High Courts," *Journal of Negro History* (1946).

Scott, Kenneth. "The Slave Insurrection in New York in 1712," *New York Historical Society Quarterly* (1961).

*Stampp, Kenneth. *The Peculiar Institution* (1956).

Starobin, Robert and Tomish, Dale. "Black Liberation Historiography," *Radical America* (1968).

Still, William. *The Underground Railroad* (1883).

Stuckey, Sterling. "Remembering Denmark Vesey," *Negro Digest* (1966).

Talley, Thomas D. *Negro Folk Rhymes* (1968).

*Wade, Richard C. *Slavery in the Cities* (1964).

———. "The Vesey Plot: A Reconsideration," *Journal of Negro Hisory* (1964).

Ward, Samuel Ringgold. *Autobiography of a Fugitive Slave* (1855).

Wax, Darold. "Negro Resistance to the Early American Slave Trade," *Journal of Negro History* (1966).

Wish, Harvey. "American Slave Insurrections before 1861," *Journal of Negro History* (1937).

*Wolfe, Bernard. "Uncle Remus and the Malevolent Rabbit," in Lawrence W. Levine and Robert Middlekauf, eds. *The National Temper* (1968).

Woodson, Carter G., ed. *The Mind of the Negro as Reflected by Letters Written during the Crisis, 1800–1860* (1926).

---

* Available in paperback.

Chapter Two

The African Slave Trade

SECTION 1. INSTRUMENTS OF TORTURE ON SLAVE SHIPS

There was no more dedicated nor influential abolitionist than the Englishman, Thomas Clarkson. Son of a Cambridgeshire clergyman, Clarkson first perceived the evils of the slave trade as a twenty-five-year-old student at Cambridge when, hearing of a prize for the best essay on the subject, "Is it lawful to make slaves of others against their will?" he did the necessary research to write a winning paper. Shortly thereafter, he believed, God commissioned him to take up the cause of abolishing the slave trade as his life's work. Over the next years Clarkson became, in the words of the poet Coleridge, "a moral steam-engine," being one of the founders of the Society for the Abolition of the Slave Trade. He compiled for publication vast amounts of information damaging to the case for slave trading, in the process interviewing seamen, merchants, ship's doctors and others at English slaving ports. He also collected the various instruments of torture used on slave ships, here described by him, along with his observations of the African's reaction to enslavement.

Description by Thomas Clarkson*

There were specimens of articles in Liverpool which I entirely overlooked at Bristol, and which, I believe, I should have overlooked here also had it not been for seeing them at a window in a shop. I mean those of different iron instruments used in this cruel traffic. I bought a pair of iron handcuffs with which the men slaves are confined. The right-hand wrist of one, and the left of another, are almost brought into contact by these, and fastened together by a little bolt with a small padlock at the end of it. I bought also a pair of shackles for the legs. The right ancle of one man is fastened to the left of another by similar means. I bought these, not because it was difficult to conceive how the unhappy victims of this execrable trade were confined, but to show the fact that they were so. For what was the inference from it, but that they did not leave their own country willingly; that when they were in the holds of the slave vessels, they were not in the Elysium which had been represented; and that there was a fear either that they would make their escape or punish their oppressors. I bought also a thumb-screw at this shop. The thumbs are put into this instrument through the two circular holes at the top of it. By turning a key, a bar rises up by a screw, and the pressure upon them becomes painful. By turning it further, you may make the blood start from the ends of them. By taking the key away, you leave the tortured person in agony, without any means of extricating himself or of being extricated by others. This screw, as I was informed, was applied by way of punishment in case of obstinacy in the slaves, or for any other reputed offence, at the discretion of the captain. At the same place I bought another instrument which I saw. It was called a speculum oris. This instrument is known among surgeons, having been invented to assist them in wrenching open the mouth as in the case of a locked jaw. But it had got into use in this trade. On asking the seller of the instruments on what occasion it was used there, he replied that the slaves were frequently so sulky as to shut their mouths against all sustenance, and this with a determination to die; and that it was necessary their mouths should be forced open to throw in nutriment, that they who had purchased them might incur no loss by their death.

---

* Reprinted from Gomer Williams, *History of the Liverpool Privateers* (London, 1897), pp. 532–533, with minor typographical changes.

SECTION 2. AN EX-SLAVE'S VIEW

Observations on the slave trade from the perspective of the enslaved African are presented by Olaudah Equiano, or, as an owner renamed him, Gustavus Vassa. Born around 1745 in the kingdom of Benin, he was the son of a village elder and slave owner; but he was kidnapped at an early age and eventually became a slave on a Virginia plantation. Subsequently he was bought by a British officer and then by a Philadelphia merchant who permitted him to purchase his freedom. Once free, he went to England where he took up the antislavery cause, in the course of his activities presenting a petition to abolish the slave trade to Parliament in 1790. The year before had appeared his memoirs *The Interesting Narrative of the Life of Olaudah Equiano, or Gustavus Vassa.* In these selections, Equiano describes two recurrent modes of resistance on slave ships — refusal to eat and jumping ship.

Equiano's Travels*

I now saw myself deprived of all chance of returning to my native country or even the least glimpse or hope of gaining the shore, which I now considered as friendly; and I even wished for my former slavery in preference to my present situation, which was filled with horrors of every kind, still heightened by my ignorance of what I was to undergo. I was not long suffered to indulge my grief; I was soon put down under the decks, and there I received such a salutation in my nostrils as I had never experienced in my life: so that with the loathsomeness of the stench and crying together, I became so sick and low that I was not able to eat, nor had I the least desire to taste anything. I now wished for the last friend, death, to relieve me; but soon, to my grief, two of the white men offered me eatables, and on my refusing to eat, one of them held me fast by the hands and laid me across I think the windlass, and tied my feet while the other flogged me severely. I had never experienced anything of this kind before, and although, not being used to the water, I naturally feared that element the first time I saw it, yet nevertheless could I have got over the nettings I would have jumped over the side, but I could not; and be-

* From Olaudah Equiano, *Equiano's Travels: The Interesting Narrative of the Life of Olaudah Equiano or Gustavus Vassa the African,* abridged and edited by Paul Edwards (New York, 1967), pp. 26–30.

sides, the crew used to watch us very closely who were not chained down to the decks, lest we should leap into the water; and I have seen some of these poor African prisoners most severely cut for attempting to do so, and hourly whipped for not eating. This indeed was often the case with myself.

.   .   .   .

One day, when we had a smooth sea and moderate wind, two of my wearied countrymen who were chained together (I was near them at the time), preferring death to such a life of misery, somehow made through the nettings and jumped into the sea: immediately another quite dejected fellow, who on account of his illness was suffered to be out of irons, also followed their example; and I believe many more would very soon have done the same if they had not been prevented by the ship's crew, who were instantly alarmed. Those of us that were the most active were in a moment put down under the deck, and there was such a noise and confusion amongst the people of the ship as I never heard before, to stop her and get the boat out to go after the slaves. However two of the wretches were drowned, but they got the other and afterwards flogged him unmercifully for thus attempting to prefer death to slavery.

SECTION 3. SLAVE MUTINIES

By far the worst of the hazards of the slave trade was the slave mutiny, which occurred mainly while ships lay at African anchor but also, not uncommonly, on the high seas. Some fifty-five mutinies have been definitely recorded for the years 1699–1845, and casual citations make mention of more than a hundred others. Two men who knew well the dangers of such outbreaks were the slave company agent Francis Moore and the slaving captain William Snelgrave. Moore was dispatched in 1735 by the Royal African Company, an English chartered company which at that time held its country's monopoly on the slave trade, to head up its operation at the mouth of the Gambia River. Among his many duties, Moore took charge of the slave stockade there, inspected the work of the other agents ("factors") in the region, carried on diplomatic relations with native chieftains, and made trips as far inland as three hundred miles to secure slaves. In his book, *Travels Into the Inland Parts of Africa* (1738), Moore reflects briefly on some advantages to the slaves of revolting in African waters rather than at sea, and, further along, reports the grisly consequences of a slave mutiny.

Captain William Snelgrave, slave trading along the Guinea Coast in the early eighteenth century, was involved in three slave mutinies. In the long section reproduced below, Snelgrave vividly recounts two of the mutinies, revealing at the same time the combined naivete, caution, and cruelty that characterized many slave traders as well as slave-owners.

Francis Moore in Africa*

All the Time he [the slave-ship captain] lies there he runs the Hazard of the Sickness and Rebellion of those Slaves he already has, they being apter to rise in a Harbour than when out at Sea; since if they once get Masters of a Ship in the River, their Escape to Shore is almost certain by running the Ship aground; but at Sea it is otherwise, for if they should surprize a Ship there, as they cannot navigate her they must have the Assistance of the White Men or perish. Besides, whilst the Ships lie in the River, the Crews are apt to be sick, and consequently not able to guard their Slaves; of which several Instances have been, and Ships lost thereby.

. . . .

On the 5th, in the Evening, I received Advice that Capt. Williams, Master of a Brigantine trading about Joar, having bought a few Slaves and not looking well to them, they mutiny'd, rose, and killed a great Part of the Ship's Crew; the Captain himself had his Fingers cut by them in a miserable Manner, and it was with great Difficulty he escaped being killed, which he did in swimming ashore, by which means he got safe to James Fort, where he was kindly received by the Governor, and took his Passage to England along with Captain Clarke in the Tryal Snow; as did likewise our third Chief Merchant, Mr. Thomas Harrison, whose Brother John died at Tancrowall the very day that he embarked from James Fort.

---

* Reprinted with minor typographical changes from Francis Moore, *Travels into the Inland Parts of Africa* (London, 1738), pp. 81, 156.

The Account of Captain Snelgrave*

I have been several Voyages when there has been no Attempt made by our Negroes to mutiny; which, I believe, was owing chiefly to their being kindly used and to my Officers' Care in keeping a good Watch. But sometimes we meet with stout stubborn People amongst them, who are never to be made easy; and these are generally some of the Cormantines, a Nation of the Gold Coast. I went in the year 1721, in the *Henry* of London, a Voyage to that part of the Coast, and bought a good many of these People. We were obliged to secure them very well in Irons and watch them narrowly: Yet they nevertheless mutinied, tho' they had little prospect of succeeding. I lay at that time near a place called Mumfort on the Gold Coast, having near five hundred Negroes on board, three hundred of which were Men. Our Ship's Company consisted of fifty white People, all in health: And I had very good Officers; so that I was very easy in all respects.

After we had secured these People, I called the Linguists and ordered them to bid the Men-Negroes between Decks be quiet (for there was a great noise amongst them). On their being silent, I asked "What had induced them to mutiny?" They answered, "I was a great Rogue to buy them, in order to carry them away from their own Country, and that they were resolved to regain their Liberty if possible." I replied "That they had forfeited their Freedom before I bought them, either by Crimes or by being taken in War, according to the Custom of their Country; and they being now my Property, I was resolved to let them feel my Resentment if they abused my Kindness: Asking at the same time, Whether they had been ill used by the white Men, or had wanted for any thing the Ship afforded?" To this they replied, "They had nothing to complain of." Then I observed to them, "That if they should gain their Point and escape to the Shore, it would be no Advantage to them, because their Countrymen would catch them and sell them to other Ships." This served my purpose, and they seemed to be convinced of their Fault, begging, "I would forgive them, and promising for the future to be obedient and never mutiny again, if I would not punish them this time." This I readily granted, and so they went to sleep. When Daylight came we called the Men Negroes up on Deck, and examining their Irons found

---

* Elizabeth Donnan, ed., *Documents Illustrative of the History of the Slave Trade to America*, vol. 2, *The Eighteenth Century* (New York, 1965), pp. 354–360. Reprinted with minor changes in punctuation and spelling.

them all secure. So this Affair happily ended, which I was very glad of; for these People are the stoutest and most sensible Negroes on the Coast: Neither are they so weak as to imagine as others do that we buy them to eat them; being satisfied we carry them to work in our Plantations as they do in their own Country.

However, a few days after this we discovered they were plotting again, and preparing to mutiny. For some of the Ringleaders proposed to one of our Linguists, If he could procure them an Ax they would cut the Cables the Ship rid by [was anchored to] in the night; and so on her driving (as they imagined) ashore they should get out of our hands and then would become his Servants as long as they lived.

For the better understanding of this I must observe here that these Linguists are Natives and Freemen of the Country, whom we hire on account of their speaking good English during the time we remain trading on the Coast; and they are likewise Brokers between us and the black Merchants.

This Linguist was so honest as to acquaint me with what had been proposed to him, and advised me to keep a strict Watch over the Slaves: For tho' he had represented to them the same as I had done on their mutinying before, that they would all be catch'd again and sold to other Ships, in case they could carry their Point and get on Shore, yet it had no effect upon them.

This gave me a good deal of Uneasiness. For I knew several Voyages had proved unsuccessful by Mutinies; as they occasioned either the total loss of the Ships and the white Men's Lives; or at least by rendering it absolutely necessary to kill or wound a great number of the Slaves in order to prevent a total Destruction. Moreover, I knew many of these Cormantine Negroes despised Punishment and even Death itself: It having often happened at Barbadoes and other Islands that on their being any ways hardly dealt with, to break them of their Stubbornness in refusing to work, twenty or more have hang'd themselves at a time in a Plantation. However, about a Month after this, a sad Accident happened that brought our Slaves to be more orderly and put them in a better Temper: And it was this. On our going from Mumfort to Annamaboe, which is the principal port on the Gold Coast, I met there with another of my Owner's Ships, called the *Elizabeth*. One Captain Thompson that commanded her was dead; as also his chief Mate: Moreover the Ship had afterwards been taken to Cape Lahoe on the windward Coast, by Roberts the Pirate, with whom several of the Sailors belonging to her had entered. However, some of the Pirates had hindered the Cargoe's being plundered, and obtained that the Ship should be restored to the second Mate: Telling him, "They did it out of respect to the generous Character his Owner bore, in doing good to poor Sailors."

When I met with this Vessel I had almost disposed of my Ship's Cargo; and the *Elizabeth* being under my Direction, I acquainted the second Mate, who then commanded her, That I thought it for our Owner's Interest to take the Slaves from on board him, being about 120, into my Ship and then go off the Coast; and that I would deliver him at the same time the Remains of my Cargo, for him to dispose of with his own after I was sailed. This he readily complied with, but told me, "He feared his Ship's Company would mutiny, and oppose my taking the Slaves from him": And indeed, they came at that instant in a Body on the Quarter-deck; where one spoke for the rest, telling me plainly, "they would not allow the Slaves to be taken out by me." I found by this they had lost all respect for their present Commander, who indeed was a weak Man. However, I calmly asked the reason, "Why they offered to oppose my taking the Slaves?" To which they answered, "I had no business with them." On this I desired the Captain to send to his Scrutore [writing desk] for the Book of Instructions Captain Thompson had received from our Owner; and he read to them at my request that Part in which their former Captain or his Successor (in case of Death) was to follow my Orders. Hereupon they all cried out, "they should [be forced to] remain a great while longer on the Coast to purchase more Slaves if I took these from them, which they were resolved to oppose." I answered, "That such of the Ship's Company as desired it I would receive on board my own [ship], where they should have the same Wages they had at present on board the *Elizabeth*, and I would send some of my own People to supply their Places." This so reasonable an Offer was refused, one of the Men who was the Ship's Cooper telling me that the Slaves had been on board a long time, and they had great Friendship with them: therefore they would keep them. I asked him, "Whether he had ever been on the Coast of Guinea before? He replied no. Then I told him, "I supposed he had not by his way of talking, and advised him not to rely on the Friendship of the Slaves, which he might have reason to repent of when too late." And 'tis remarkable this very person was killed by them the next Night, as shall be presently related.

So finding that reasoning with these Men was to no Purpose, I told them, "When I came with my Boats to fetch the Slaves, they should find me as resolute to chastise such of them as should dare to oppose me as I had been condescending to convince them by arguing calmly." So I took my leave of their Captain, telling him, "I would come the next Morning to finish the Affair."

But that very Night, which was near a month after the Mutiny on board of us at Mumfort, the Moon shining now very bright, as it did then, we heard about ten a Clock two or three Musquets fired on board the *Elizabeth*. Upon that I ordered all our Boats to be manned, and having secured everything in our Ship to prevent our Slaves from mutinying, I went myself in our Pinnace (the other Boats following me) on board the *Elizabeth*. In our way we saw two Negroes swimming from her, but before we could reach them with our Boats, some Sharks rose from the bottom, and tore them in Pieces. We came presently along the side of the Ship, where we found two Men-Negroes holding by a Rope, with their heads just above water; they were afraid, it seems, to swim from the Ship's side, having seen their Companions devoured just before by the Sharks. These two Slaves we took into our Boat, and then went into the Ship where we found the Negroes very quiet, and all under Deck; but the Ship's Company was on the Quarter-deck, in a great Confusion, saying, "The Cooper [barrel-maker], who had been placed centry at the Fore-hatch way over the Men-Negroes, was, they believed, kill'd by them." I was surprized to hear this, wondring that these cowardly fellows, who had so vigorously opposed my taking the Slaves out a few hours before, had not Courage enough to venture forward to save their Ship-mate, but had secured themselves by shutting the Quarter-deck door where they all stood with Arms in their Hands. So I went to the fore-part of the Ship with some of my People, and there we found the Cooper lying on his back quite dead, his Scull being cleft asunder with a Hatchet that lay by him. At the sight of this I called for the Linguist, and bid him ask the Negroes between Decks, "Who had killed the white Man?" They answered, "They knew nothing of the matter; for there had been no design of mutinying among them": Which upon Examination we found true; for above one hundred of the Negroes then on board, being bought to the Windward [on the earlier part of the ship's voyage], did not understand a word of the Gold-Coast Language and so had not been in the Plot. But this Mutiny was contrived by a few Cormantee-Negroes, who had been purchased about two or three days before. At last, one of the two Men-Negroes we had taken up along the Ship side, impeached his Companion, and he readily confessed he had kill'd the Cooper, with no other View, but that he and his Country-men might escape undiscovered by swimming on Shore. For on their coming upon Deck, they observed that all the white Men set to watch were asleep; and having found the Cook's Hatchet by the Fire-place, he took it up, not designing then to do any Mischief with it; but passing by the Cooper, who was century [sentry] and he [who was] beginning

to awake, the Negroe rashly struck him on the head with it and then
jump'd overboard. Upon this frank Confession the white Men would
have cut him to Pieces; but I prevented it and carried him to my own
Ship. Early the next morning, I went on board the *Elizabeth* with my
Boats and sent away all the Negroes then in her into my own Ship,
not one of the other Ship's Company offering to oppose it. Two of
them, the Carpenter and Steward, desired to go with me, which I
readily granted; and by way of Security for the future success of the
Voyage, I put my chief Mate and four of my under Officers (with their
own Consent) on board the *Elizabeth*; and they arrived five Months
after this at Jamaica, having disposed of most part of the Cargo.

After having sent the Slaves out of the *Elizabeth,* as I have just
now mentioned, I went on board my own Ship; and there being then
in the Road of Anamaboe eight sail of Ships besides us, I sent an
Officer in my Boat to the Commanders of them, "To desire their
Company on board my Ship, because I had an Affair of great Consequence to communicate to them." Soon after, most of them were
pleased to come; and I having acquainted them with the whole Matter,
and they having also heard the Negroe's Confession, "That he had
killed the white Man," They unanimously advised me to put him to
death; arguing, "That Blood required Blood, by all Laws both divine
and human; especially as there was in this Case the clearest Proof,
namely the Murderer's Confession: Moreover this would in all probability prevent future Mischiefs; for by publickly executing this Person
at the Ship's Fore-yard Arm, the Negroes on board their Ships would
see it; and as they were very much disposed to mutiny, it might prevent them from attempting it." These Reasons, with my being in the
same Circumstances, made me comply.

Accordingly we acquainted the Negroe, that he was to die in an
hour's time for murdering the white Man. He answered, "He must
confess it was a rash Action in him to kill him; but he desired me to
consider, that if I put him to death, I should lose all the Money I
had paid for him." To this I bid the Interpreter reply, "That tho' I
knew it was customary in his Country to commute for Murder by a
Sum of Money, yet it was not so with us; and he should find that I
had no regard to my Profit in this respect: For as soon as an Hour-Glass,
just then turned, was run out, he should be put to death"; At which I
observed he showed no Concern.

Hereupon the other commanders went on board their respective
Ships, in order to have all their Negroes upon Deck at the time of
Execution, and to inform them of the occasion of it. The Hour-Glass

being run out, the Murderer was carried on the Ship's Forecastle, where he had a Rope fastened under his Arms, in order to be hoisted up to the Fore-yard Arm, to be shot to death. This some of his Country-men observing, told him (as the Linguist informed me afterwards) "That they would not have him to be frightened; for it was plain I did not design to put him to death, otherwise the Rope would have been put about his neck, to hang him." For it seems they had no thought of his being shot; judging he was only to be hoisted up to the Yard-arm, in order to scare him: But they immediately saw the con-trary; for as soon as he was hoisted up, ten white Men who were placed behind the Barricado on the Quarter-deck fired their Musquets, and instantly killed him. This struck a sudden Damp upon our Negroe-Men, who thought that on account of my Profit I would not have executed him.

The Body being cut down upon the Deck, the Head was cut off, and thrown overboard. This last part was done to let our Negroes see that all who offended thus should be served in the same manner. For many of the Blacks believe that if they are put to death and not dismembred, they shall return again to their own Country after they are thrown overboard. But neither the Person that was executed nor his Countrymen of Cormantee (as I understood afterwards) were so weak as to believe any such thing; tho' many I had on board from other Countries had that Opinion.

When the Execution was over, I ordered the Linguist to acquaint the Men-Negroes, "That now they might judge, no one that killed a white Man should be spared": And I thought proper now to acquaint them once for all, "That if they attempted to mutiny again, I should be obliged to punish the Ringleaders with death, in order to prevent further Mischief." Upon this they all promised to be obedient, and I assured them they should be kindly used, if they kept their Promise: which they faithfully did. For we sailed two days after from Anamaboe for Jamaica; and tho' they were on board nearly four Months, from our going off the Coast till they were sold at that Island, they never gave us the least reason to be jealous of them; which doubtless was owing to the execution of the white Man's Murderer.

Chapter Three

The Afro-American Culture

SECTION 1. A STRAIGHT LICK WITH A CROOKED STICK — TALES

The Afro-American slave culture produced an impressive body of mother wit, aphorisms, and folktales. A number of Negro writers and commentators, along with a few interested whiles, have long pointed out that many of these materials were attempts at "hitting a straight lick with a crooked stick," that is, putting one over on the white man, in a subtle, partially disguised way. The three stories selected for reproduction here, highlight this theme. The first two, presented by the Negro writers Langston Hughes and Arna Bontemps, show how quick-wittedness was a survival as well as a resistance mechanism. The third is the tale of Brer Rabbit's final violent encounter with Brer Fox ("The Sad Fate of Mister Fox"). The character of Uncle Remus and the setting — the kindly old Negro retainer seated in his cabin back of the "big house" with the little white boy, son of "Miss Sally" and "Mars John," on his knee — were the invention of Joel Chandler Harris, a white Atlanta newspaperman, in the early 1880's. But when Uncle Remus begins to tell his stories, the Negro takes over, for Harris got his material from the tales of former slaves. The evidence suggests that Harris did not fully comprehend the malice beneath the surface of the stories, the vengeful grimace beneath the Uncle Remus–Uncle Tom grin.

Dreaming*

Master Jim Turner, an unusually good-natured master, had a
fondness for telling long stories woven out of what he claimed to be
his dreams, and especially did he like to "swap" dreams with Ike, a
witty slave who was a house servant. Every morning he would set
Ike to telling about what he had dreamed the night before. It always
seemed, however, that the master could tell the best dream tale, and
Ike had to admit that he was beaten most of the time.

One morning, when Ike entered the master's room to clean it, he
found the master just preparing to get out of bed. "Ike," he said, "I
certainly did have a strange dream last night."

"Sez, yuh did, Massas, sez yuh did?" answered Ike. "Lemme
hyeah it."

"All right," replied the master. "It was like this: I dreamed I
went to Nigger Heaven last night, and saw there a lot of garbage,
some old torn-down houses, a few old broken-down, rotten fences,
the muddiest, sloppiest streets I ever saw, and a big bunch of ragged,
dirty Negroes walking around."

"Umph, umph, Massa," said Ike, "yuh sho' musta et de same t'ing
Ah did las' night, 'case Ah dreamed Ah went up ter de white man's
paradise, an' de streets wuz all ob gol' an' silvah, and dey wuz lots o'
milk an' honey dere, an' putty pearly gates, but dey wuzn't uh soul
in de whole place."

Uncle Israel

Every week on the Hunter plantation five or six chickens would
be missing, and the master couldn't find out what had become of
them. At length he started a thorough investigation. After a good
deal of questioning among the slaves, he found that Uncle Israel's
wife had recently made some feather pillows and that chicken feathers
had been seen under Uncle Israel's cabin a few days before.

With this information, the master laid his trap. One evening a
strange white man driving a wobbly old buggy with a chicken coop
tied on the back end of it halted at Uncle Israel's cabin. He was a
chicken buyer, he said, and was paying fancy prices. Uncle Israel was
not long in suggesting that he might have a few very fat chickens to
sell.

---

* This tale and the next are from *The Book of Negro Folklore*, eds. Langston
Hughes and Arna Bontemps (New York, 1959), pp. 71–72.

"All right," said the stranger, "bring them out."

"No, sah, no, sah," explained Uncle Israel, "Ah cain't ketch 'em till da'k."

The stranger went on to say that he didn't much want to hang around the plantation and be seen by Mr. Hunter and finally asked Uncle Israel point-blank where he was going to get his chickens.

"Wal, Ah tell yuh," chuckled Uncle Israel. "Ah's got uh hoodo on dem chickens up dar in Massa's hen-house. Dey comes into mah sack after da'k lak crows flyin' to de roost-tree in de ebenin'!"

"Aw," sneered the stranger, "you know you are afraid to go into your master's hen-house."

"Yuh jes' wait an' see," answered Uncle Israel. He was all eagerness. "Why, two of dem pullets flewed right into mah ol' 'oman's stew kittle las' night."

"You don't say," explained the stranger in a changed tone. "Do you know who I am?"

"No, sah, Boss, 'ceptin' yuh's a chicken buyah. Who else is yuh?"

"I'm the biggest constable in this county," answered the stranger.

"Sez yuh is, Boss?" said Uncle Israel. "Wal, Ah'll decla'. An' don' yuh know who Ah is? Ain't Massa and de oberseeah tol' yuh who Ah is? Wal, Ah's de bigges' liah in dis county."

The Sad Fate of Mr. Fox*

"Now, den," said Uncle Remus, with unusual gravity, as soon as the little boy, by taking his seat, announced that he was ready for the evening's entertainment to begin; "now, den, dish yer tale w'at I'm agwine ter gin you is de las' row er stumps, sho. Dish yer's whar ole Brer Fox los' his breff, en he ain't fine it no mo' down ter dis day."

"Did he kill himself, Uncle Remus?" the little boy asked, with a curious air of concern.

"Hole on dar, honey!" the old man exclaimed, with a great affectation of alarm; "hole on dar! Wait! Gimme room! I don't wanter tell tell you no story, en ef you keep shovin' me forred, I mout git some er de facks mix up 'mong deyse'f. You gotter gimme room en you gotter gimme time."

The little boy had no other premature questions to ask, and, after a pause, Uncle Remus resumed:

---

* From Joel Chandler Harris, *Uncle Remus: His Songs and Sayings* (New York, 1921), pp. 168–174.

"Well, den, one day Brer Rabbit go ter Brer Fox house, he did, en he put up mighty po' mouf. He say his ole 'oman sick, en his chilluns cole, en de fier done gone out. Brer Fox, he feel bad 'bout dis, en he tuck'n s'ply Brer Rabbit widder chunk er fier. Brer Rabbit see Brer Fox cookin' some nice beef, en his mouf 'gun ter water, but he take de fier, he did, en he put out to'rds home; but present'y yer he come back, en he say de fier done gone out. Brer Fox 'low dat he want er invite ter dinner, but he don't say nuthin', en bimeby Brer Rabbit he up'n say, sezee:

" 'Brer Fox, whar you git so much nice beef?' sezee, en den Brer Fox he up'n 'spon', sezee:

" 'You come ter my house ter-morrer ef yo' fokes ain't too sick, en I kin show you whar you kin git plenty beef mo' nicer dan dish yer,' sezee:

"Well, sho nuff, der nex' day fotch Brer Rabbit, en Brer Fox say, sezee:

" 'Der's a man down yander by Miss Meadows's w'at got heap er fine cattle, en he gotter cow name Bookay,' sezee, 'en you des go en say *Bookay*, en she'll open her mouf en you kin jump in en git as much meat ez you kin tote," sez Brer Fox, sezee.

" 'Well, I'll go 'long,' sez Brer Rabbit, sezee, 'en you kin jump fus' en den I'll come follerin' atter,' sezee.

"Wid dat day put out, en dey went promernadin' 'roun' 'mong de cattle, dey did, twel bimeby dey struck up wid de one dey wuz atter. Brer Fox, he up, he did, en holler *Bookay*, en de cow flung 'er mouf wide open. Sho nuff, in dey jump, en w'en dey got dar, Brer Fox, he say, sezee:

" 'You kin cut mos' ennywheres, Brer Rabbit, but don't cut 'roun' de haslett,' sezee.

"Den Brer Rabbit, he holler back, he did: 'I'm a gitten me out a roas'n-piece'; sezee.

" 'Roas'n, er bakin', er fryin',' sez Brer Fox, sezee, 'don't git too nigh de haslett,' sezee.

"Dey cut en dey kyarved, en dey kyarved en dey cut, en w'iles dey wuz cuttin' en kyarvin', en slashin' 'way, Brer Rabbit, he tuck'n hacked inter de haslett, en wid dat down fell de cow dead.

" 'Now, den,' scz Brer Fox, 'we er gone, sho,' sezee.

" 'W'at we gwine do?' sez Brer Rabbit, sezee.

" 'I'll git in de maul,' sez Brer Fox, 'en you'll jump in de gall,' sezee.

"Nex' mownin' yer cum de man w'at de cow b'long ter, an he ax who kill Bookay. Nobody don't say nuthin'. Den de man say he'll cut 'er open en see, en den he whirl in, en twan't no time 'fo' he had 'er intruls spread out. Brer Rabbit, he crope out'n de gall, en say, sezee:

" 'Mister Man! Oh, Mister Man! I'll tell you who kill yo' cow. You look in de maul, en dar you'll fine 'im,' sezee.

"Wid dat de man tuck a stick and lam down on de maul so hard dat he kill Brer Fox stone-dead. W'en Brer Rabbit see Brer Fox wuz laid out fer good, he make like he mighty sorry, en he up'n ax de man fer Brer Fox head. Man say he ain't keerin', en den Brer Rabbit tuck'n brung it ter Brer Fox house. Dar he see ole Miss Fox, en he tell 'er dat he done fotch her some nice beef w'at 'er ole man sont 'er, but she ain't gotter look at it twel she go ter eat it.

"Brer Fox son wuz name Tobe, en Brer Rabbit tell Tobe fer ter keep still w'iles his manny cook de nice beef w'at his daddy sont 'im. Tobe he wuz mighty hongry, en he look in de pot he did w'iles de cookin' wuz gwine on, en dar he see his daddy head, en wid dat he sot up a howl en tole his mammy. Miss Fox, she git mighty mad w'en she fine she cookin' her ole man head, en she call up de dogs, she did, en sickt em on Brer Rabbit; en ole Miss Fox en Tobe en de dogs, dey push Brer Rabbit so close dat he hatter take a holler tree. Miss Fox, she tell Tobe fer ter stay dar en mine Brer Rabbit, w'ile she goes en git de ax, en w'en she gone, Brer Rabbit, he tole Tobe ef he go ter de branch en git 'im a drink er water dat he'll gin 'im a dollar. Tobe, he put out, he did, en bring some water in his hat, but by de time he got back Brer Rabbit done out en gone. Ole Miss Fox, she cut and cut twel down come de tree, but no Brer Rabbit dar. Den she lay de blame on Tobe, en she say she gwineter lash 'im, en Tobe, he put out en run, de ole 'oman atter 'im. Bimeby, he come up wid Brer Rabbit, en sot down fer to tell 'im how 'twuz, en w'iles dey wuz a settin' dar, yer come ole Miss Fox a slippin' up en grab um bofe. Den she tell um w'at she gwine do. Brer Rabbit she gwineter kill, en Tobe she gwineter lam ef its de las' ack. Den Brer Rabbit sez, sezee:

" 'Ef you please, ma'am, Miss Fox, lay me on de grindstone en groun' off my nose so I can't smell no mo' w'en I'm dead.'

"Miss Fox, she tuck dis ter be a good idee, en she fotch bofe un um ter de grindstone, en set um up on it so dat she could groun' off Brer Rabbit nose. Den Brer Rabbit, he up'n say, sezee:

" 'Ef you please, ma'am, Miss Fox, Tobe he kin turn de' handle w'iles you goes atter some water fer ter wet de grinestone,' sezee.

"Co'se, soon'z Brer Rabbit see Miss Fox go atter de water, he jump down en put out, en dis time he git clean away."

"And was that the last of the Rabbit, too, Uncle Remus?" the little boy asked, with something like a sigh.

"Don't push me too close, honey," responded the old man; "don't shove me up in no cornder. I don't wanter tell you no stories. Some say dat Brer Rabbit's ole 'oman died fum eatin' some pizen-weed, en dat Brer Rabbit married ole Miss Fox, en some say not. Some tells one tale en some tells nudder; some say dat fum dat time forrer'd de Rabbits en de Foxes make frien's en stay so; some say dey kep on quollin'. Hit look like it mixt. Let dem tell you w'at knows. Dat w'at I years you gits it straight like I yeard it."

There was a long pause, which was finally broken by the old man: "Hit's 'gin de rules fer you ter be noddin' yer, honey. Bimeby you'll drap off en I'll hatter tote you up ter de big house. I hear dat baby cryin', en bimeby Miss Sally'll fly up en be a holler'n atter you."

"Oh, I wasn't asleep," the little boy replied. "I was just thinking."

"Well, dat's diffunt," said the old man. "Ef you'll clime up on my back," he continued, speaking softly, "I speck I ain't too ole fer ter be yo' hoss fum yer ter de house. Many en many's de time dat I toted yo' Unk Jeems dat away, en Mars Jeems wuz heavier sot dan w't you is."

SECTION 2. RHYMES OF FOOLING MASTER

Through the folk rhymes slaves registered their gaiety and their gloom, and all ranges of feeling in between. The following rhymes, collected from many different sources over the years, indicate that slaves enjoyed doing the master in, even if only by verse.

Judge Buzzard*

> Dere sets Jedge Buzzard en de Bench.
> Go tu'n him off wid a monkey wrench!
> Jedge Buzzard try Brer Rabbit's case;
> An' he say Brer Tarepin win dat race.
> Here sets Jedge Buzzard on de Bench.
> Knock him off wid dat monkey wrench!

---

* This and the following five rhymes are taken from Thomas W. Talley, *Negro Folk Rhymes* (Port Washington, New York, 1922), pp. 16, 25–26, 40, 48, 114, 122. Some typographical alterations.

Promises of Freedom

My ole Mistiss promise me,
W'en she died, she'd set me free.
She lived so long dat 'er head got bal',
An' she give out'n de notion a dyin' at all.

My ole Mistiss say to me:
"Sambo, I'se gwine ter set you free."
But w'en dat head git slick an' bal',
De Lawd couldn' a' killed 'er wid a big green maul.

My ole Mistiss never die,
Wid 'er nose all hooked an' skin all dry.
But my ole Miss, she's somehow gone,
An' she lef' "Uncle Sambo" a-hillin' up co'n.

Ole Mosser go an' make his Will
Fer to leave me a-plowin' ole Beck still.
  Yes, my ole Mosser promise me;
But "his papers" didn' leave me free.
A dose of pizen he'ped 'im along.
May de Devil preach 'is funer'l song.

Master Is Six Feet One Way

Mosser is six foot one way, an' free foot tudder;
An' he weigh five hunderd pound.
Britches cut so big dat dey don't suit de tailor,
An' dey don't meet half way 'round.
Mosser's coat come back to a claw-hammer p'int.
(Speak sof' or his Bloodhound'll bite us.)
His long white stockin's mighty clean an' nice,
But a liddle mo' holier dan righteous.

Nobody Looking

Well: I look dis a way, an' I look dat a way,
    An' I heared a mighty rumblin'.
    W'en I come to find out, 'twus dad's black sow,
    A-rootin' an' a-grumblin'.

Den: I slipped away down to de big White House.
Miss Sallie, she done gone 'way.
I popped myse'f in de rockin' chear,
An' I rocked myse'f all day.

Now: I looked dis a way, and' I looked dat a way,
An' I didn' see nobody in here.
I jes run'd my head in de coffee pot,
An' I drink'd up all o' de beer.

I'll Eat When I'm Hungry

I'll eat when I'se hongry,
An' I'll drink when I'se dry;
An' if de whitefolks don't kill me,
I'll live till I die.

In my liddle log cabin,
Ever since I'se been born;
Dere hain't been no nothin'
'Cept dat hard salt parch corn.

But I knows whar's a henhouse,
An' de tucky he charve;
An' if ole Mosser don't kill me,
I cain't never starve.

Parody on "Reign, Master Jesus, Reign!"

Oh rain! Oh rain! Oh rain, "good" Mosser!
Rain, Mosser, rain! Rain hard!
Rain flour an' lard an' a big hog head
Down in my back yard.

An' w'en you comes down to my cabin,
Come down by de corn fiel'.
If you cain't bring me a piece o' meat,
Den bring me a peck o' meal.

Oh rain! Oh rain! Oh rain, "good" Mosser!
Dat good rain gives mo' rest.
"What d'you say? You Nigger, dar!"
"Wet ground grows grass best."

The Funniest Things*

Charlie could make up songs 'bout de funnies' things. One day Charlie saw ole Marsa comin' home wid a keg of whiskey on his ole mule. Cuttin' 'cross de plowed field, de ole mule slipped an' Marsa come tumblin' off. Marsa didn't know Charlie saw him, an' Charlie didn't say nothin'. But soon arter a visitor come an' Marsa called Charlie to de house to show off what he knew. Marsa say, "Come here, Charlie, an' sing some rhymes fo' Mr. Henson." "Don't know no new ones, Marsa," Charlie answered. "Come on, you black rascal, give me a rhyme fo' my company—one he ain't heard." So Charlie say, "All right, Marsa, I give you a new one effen you promise not to whup me." Marsa promised, an' den Charlie sung de rhyme he done made up in his haid 'bout Marsa:

> Jackass rared
> Jackass pitch
> Throwed ole Marsa in de ditch.

Well, Marsa got mad as a hornet, but he didn't whup Charlie, not dat time anyway. An' chile, don' you know us used to act de flo' to dat dere song? Mind you, never would sing it when Marsa was roun', but when he wasn't we'd swing all roun' de cabin singin' 'bout how old Marsa fell off de mule's back. Charlie had a bunch of verses:

> Jackass stamped
> Jackass neighed
> Throwed ole Marsa on his haid.

Don' recoll' all dat smart slave made up. But ev'ybody sho' bus' dey sides laughin' when Charlie sung de las' verse:

> Jackass stamped
> Jackass hupped
> Marsa hear you slave, you sho' git whupped.

Fooling Master†

> I fooled Old Master seven years,
>   Fooled the overseer three.
> Hand me down my banjo,
>   And I'll tickle your bel-lee.

---

* W.P.A. Federal Writer's Project, *The Negro in Virginia* (New York, 1940), pp. 94–95.

† From B. A. Botkin, ed., *Lay My Burden Down: A Folk History of Slavery* (Chicago, 1965), p. 3.

White Man Gets the Money*

When visitors were at "Poplar Farm," Dr. Gaines would frequently call in Cato to sing a song or crack a joke, for the amusement of the company. On one occasion, requesting the servant to give a toast, at the same time handing the Negro a glass of wine, the latter took the glass, held it up, looked at it, began to show his ivory [teeth] and said:

> De big bee flies high,
>> De little bee makes de honey,
> De black man raise de cotton,
>> An' de white man gets de money.

SECTION 3. SPIRITUALS AND SECULAR SONGS

The essay in Chapter I explored the idea that the songs of the slaves were vital modes of expression and communication for an oppressed people. In this section are included a number of songs that bear an obvious and moving relation to the slave situation.

Serving as the colonel of a black regiment in the Union Army during the Civil War, the white New England abolitionist Thomas Wentworth Higginson noted down a number of his soldiers' songs which came out of their experience as slaves. The first three selections below are taken from his fascinating book, *Army Life in a Black Regiment*, originally published in 1869.

Harriet Tubman, reputed to have brought out more than three hundred slaves on nineteen forays into the South, used the spirituals with their double meanings in her work. When she came upon the slave cabins she would alert the residents through song that she was prepared to take them to freedom: "When dat ar chariot comes, I'm gwine to lebe you, I'm boun' for de promised land, Frien's, I'm gwine to lebe you." "Bound for the Promised Land," and "One More Soul Got Safe" were sung by Harriet's fugitive group — the first on the way to Canada and the second once they had arrived.

"Sam's Song," the following piece, was presented as a slave song by abolitionist William Wells Brown, in his novel, *Clotel: or, the Presi-*

---

* From William Wells Brown, *My Southern Home* (Boston, 1880), p. 66.

dent's Daughter. The first novel by an American Negro, the book was published in London in 1853 and in the United States two years later.

The next selection has an interesting history. During the Civil War a Hudson Valley minister, John Forsyth, wrote to author Benson John Lossing, telling him about a freedom hymn sung by Negro slaves on an island near Charleston, South Carolina, at the time of the War of 1812. According to the English abolitionist George Thompson, who had told the story to Forsyth, "A Hymn to Freedom," as it was called, was composed by one of the men deeply involved in planning a slave insurrection and was sung at the opening and closing of the nightly meetings. The plot was apparently tied into the anticipated British invasion of the coast of Carolina.

Like other forms of artistic protest and resistance, the slave spirituals necessarily spoke in mysterious terms, designed to be comprehended only by the singers. The last two songs reproduced here are well known to modern Americans: "Joshua," and "Go Down, Moses." The latter, at least, was clear enough in meaning so that runaways reported that masters often forbade their slaves to sing it.

We'll Soon Be Free*

We'll soon be free,
We'll soon be free,
We'll soon be free,
    When de Lord will call us home.

My brudder, how long,
My brudder, how long,
My brudder, how long,
    'Fore we done sufferin' here?

It won't be long (*Thrice*)
    'Fore de Lord will call us home.

We'll walk de miry road (*Thrice*)
    Where pleasure never dies.

We'll walk de golden street (*Thrice*)
    Where pleasure never dies.

---

* This and the next two items are from Thomas Wentworth Higgenson, *Army Life in a Black Regiment* (East Lansing, Michigan, 1960), pp. 169–170. Some changes in spacing and punctuation.

My brudder, how long (*Thrice*)
'Fore we done sufferin' here?

We'll soon be free (*Thrice*)
When Jesus sets me free.

We'll fight for liberty (*Thrice*)
When de Lord will call us home.

Many Thousand Go

No more peck o' corn for me,
No more, no more,

No more peck o' corn for me,
Many tousand go.

No more driver's lash for me, (*Twice*)
No more, etc. . . .

No more pint o' salt for me, (*Twice*)
No more, etc. . . .

No more hundred lash for me, (*Twice*)
No more, etc. . . .

No more mistress' call for me,
No more, no more,

No more mistress' call for me,
Many tousand go.

The Driver

O, de ole nigger-driver!
O, gwine away!

Fust ting my mammy tell me,
O, gwine away!

Tell me 'bout de nigger-driver,
   O, gwine away!

Nigger-driver second devil,
   O, gwine away!

Best ting for do he driver,
   O, gwine away!

Knock he down and spoil he labor,
   O, gwine away!

Bound for the Promised Land*

I'm on the way to Canada,
   That cold and dreary land,
De sad effects of slavery,
   I can't no longer stand;
I've served my Master all my days.
   Widout a dime reward,
And now I'm forced to run away,
   To flee de lash, abroad;
Farewell, ole Master, don't think hard of me,
I'm traveling on to Canada, where all de slaves are free.

De hounds are baying on my track,
   Ole Master comes behind,
Resolved that he will bring me back,
   Before I cross the line;
I'm now embarked for yonder shore,
   Where a man's *a man* by law,
De iron horse will bear me o'er,
   To "shake de lion's paw;"
Oh, righteous Father, wilt thou not pity me,
And help me on to Canada, where all de slaves are free.

* This and the next selection are from Sarah Bradford, *Harriet Tubman: the Moses of Her People* (New York, 1961), pp. 49–52. Minor punctuation alterations.

Oh I heard Queen Victoria say,
     That if we would forsake,
Our native land of slavery,
     And come across de lake;
Dat she was standing on de shore,
     Wild arms extended wide,
To give us all a peaceful home,
     Beyond de rolling tide;
Farewell, ole Master, don't think hard of me,
I'm traveling on to Canada, where all de slaves are free.

One More Soul Got Safe

Glory to God and Jesus too,
     One more soul got safe;
Oh, go and carry the news,
     One more soul got safe.
Joe, come and look at the falls!*
     Glory to God and Jesus too,
     One more soul got safe.
Joe! it's your last chance. Come and see de falls!
     Glory to God and Jesus too,
     One more soul got safe.

Sam's Song†

Come, all my brethren, let us take a rest
     While the moon shines so brightly and clear;
Old master is dead, and left us at last,
     And has gone at the Bar to appear.
Old master has died, and lying in his grave,
     And our blood will awhile cease to flow;
He will no more trample on the neck of the slave;
     For he's gone where the slaveholders go.

(Chorus)
Hang up the shovel and the hoe—
Take down the fiddle and the bow

---

* This evidently refers to Niagara Falls, which is on the border between New York and Ontario, Canada.

† From William Wells Brown, *Clotel; or, the President's Daughter* (Philadelphia, 1855), pp. 149–150. Some typographical changes.

Old master has gone to the slaveholder's rest;
He has gone where they all ought to go.

I heard the old doctor say the other night,
    As he passed by the dining-room door—
"Perhaps the old man may live through the night,
    But I think he will die about four."
Young mistress sent me, at the peril of my life,
    For the parson to come down and pray,
For says she, "Your old master is now about to die,"
    And says I, "God speed him on his way."

(*Chorus*)
Hang up the shovel, etc. . . .

At four o'clock at morn the family was called
    Around the old man's dying bed;
And oh! but I laughed to myself when I heard
    That the old man's spirit had fled.
Mr. Carlton cried, and so did I pretend;
    Young mistress very nearly went mad;
And the old parson's groans did the heavens fairly rend;
    But I tell you I felt mighty glad.

(*Chorus*)
Hang up the shovel, etc. . . .

We'll no more be roused by the blowing of his horn,
    Our backs no longer will he score;
He no more will feed us on cotton-seeds and corn;
    For his reign of oppression is o're.
He no more will hang our children on the tree,
    To be ate by the carrion crow;
He no more will send our wives to Tennessee;
    For he's gone where the slaveholders go!

(*Chorus*)
Hang up the shovel and the hoe,
Take down the fiddle and the bow,
We'll dance and sing,
And make the forest ring,
With the fiddle and the old banjo.

A Hymn to Freedom*

Hail! all hail! ye Afric clan
Hail! ye oppressed, ye Afric band,
Who toil and sweat in Slavery bound;
(Repeated)
And when your health and strength are gone
Are left to hunger and to mourn.
Let *Independence* be your aim,
Ever mindful what 'tis worth.
Pledge your bodies for the prize
Pile them even to the skies!

(Chorus)
Firm, united let us be,
Resolved on death or liberty
As a band of Patriots joined
Peace and Plenty we shall find.

Look to Heaven with manly trust
And swear by Him that's always just
That no white foe with impious hand
(Repeated)
Shall slave your wives and daughters more
Or rob them of their virtue dear.
Be armed with valor firm and true,
Their hopes are fixed on Heaven and you
That truth and justice will prevail
And every scheme of bondage fail.

(Chorus)
Firm, united, etc. . . .

Arise! Arise! shake off your chains
Your cause is just, so Heaven ordains
To you shall Freedom be proclaimed.
(Repeated)

---

* John Hammond Moore, ed., "Hymn: A Hymn of Freedom from South Carolina, 1813," *Journal of Negro History* 50 (January, 1965), pp. 52–53. Typography changed slightly.

Raise your arms and bare your breasts,
Almighty God will do the rest.
Blow the clarion! a warlike blast!
Call every Negro from his task!
Wrest the scourge from Buckra's hand,
And drive each tyrant from the land.

(*Chorus*)
Firm, united, etc. . . .

Joshua*

Joshua fit de battle ob Jerico, Jerico, Jerico
Joshua fit de battle ob Jerico,
An' de walls come tumblin' down

You may talk about yo' king ob Gideon,
You may talk about yo' man ob Saul,
Dere's none like good ole Joshua
At de battle ob Jerico

Up to de walls ob Jerico
He marched with spear in han',
"Go blow dem ram horns" Joshua cried,
"Kase de battle am in my han'."

Den de lam' ram sheep horns begin to blow,
Trumpets begin to soun',
Joshua commanded de chillen to shout,
An' de walls come tumblin' down
Dat mornin'
Joshua fit de battle ob Jerico, Jerico, Jerico,
An' de walls come tumblin' down.

---

* This song and the next are from James Weldon Johnson and J. Rosamond Johnson, eds., *The Books of American Negro Spirituals*, 2 vols. in 1 (New York, 1969), pp. 51–53, 56–58. Some change in punctuation, as with other items.

Go Down, Moses

> Go down, Moses,
> 'Way down in Egypt land,
> Tell ole Pharaoh
> To let my people go.
> Go down, Moses,
> 'Way down in Egypt land,
> Tell ole Pharaoh,
> To let my people go.
>
> When Israel was in Egypt's land,
> Let my people go,
> Oppressed so hard they could not stand,
> Let my people go.
>
> "Thus spoke the Lord,"
> Bold Moses said:
> " 'Let my people go,
> " 'If not I'll smite your first born dead,'
> "Let my people go."
>
> Go down, Moses,
> 'Way down in Egypt land,—
> Tell ole Pharaoh
> To let my people go.
> O let my people go.

SECTION 4. SLAVE RELIGION

If the black response to religion has been "submissive, humble and obedient," as Negro scholar Benjamin Mays argued years ago in *The Negro's God*, there has been another side as well. Blacks have also responded to their religion with, in the words of a contemporary black scholar, Vincent Harding, "protest, resistance and death." Long-time slave Charles Ball explained that his religion, and the religion of others like him, was based on the idea of revolution.

Charles Ball on Religion and Revolution*

It is impossible to reconcile the mind of the native slave to the idea of living in a state of perfect equality and boundless affection with the white people. Heaven will be no heaven to him if he is not to be avenged of his enemies. I know from experience that these are the fundamental rules of his religious creed, because I learned them in the religious meetings of the slaves themselves. A favorite and kind master or mistress may now and then be admitted into heaven, but this rather as a matter of favor to the intercession of some slave than as matter of strict justice to the whites, who will by no means be of an equal rank with those who shall be raised from the depths of misery in this world.

The idea of a revolution in the conditions of the whites and the blacks is the corner-stone of the religion of the latter; and indeed, it seems to me at least to be quite natural, if not in strict accordance with the precepts of the Bible; for in that book I find it everywhere laid down that those who have possessed an inordinate portion of the good things of this world, and have lived in ease and luxury at the expense of their fellow men, will surely have to render an account of their stewardship and be punished for having withheld from others the participation of those blessings which they themselves enjoyed.

---

* Charles Ball, *Fifty Years in Chains; or, the Life of an American Slave* (Indianapolis, 1859), pp. 150–151. Punctuation altered.

Chapter Four

Day-to-Day Resistance in the Slave South

SECTION 1. THE FUGITIVE SLAVE

Abolitionist orator Samuel Ringgold Ward, himself a runaway, once commented on the "constantly present" fear of the master that his slave would take flight. Thus, "all manner of precautions" were taken by him, Ward wrote. Nevertheless, thousands did run away, whether to Louisiana and Florida or, more often, to the North and Canada. In the first selections in this chapter, two celebrated abolitionists, the Reverend J. W. C. Pennington, a Presbyterian minister in New York City and early challenger of discrimination on public conveyances, and Henry Bibb, who became a newspaper editor and booster of Canadian colonization, write of the many difficulties that confronted any bondsman who gave serious thought to fleeing the plantation.

Although most slaves chose more conventional means of running away, a number worked out ingenious disguises. Two of the most celebrated runaway make-up artists were William and Ellen Craft. In late 1848, with the light-skinned Ellen posing as a slaveowner and William as her attendant slave, the Crafts successfully made their way from Macon, Georgia, to Philadelphia. William Wells Brown, who describes their escape in the third document below, took them in hand and saw to it that they were properly exposed at abolitionist meetings throughout New England. Some time after the Crafts took up residence in England, it was rumored that they were unhappy and wished to return to Georgia and slavery, to which Ellen tartly replied with a letter to a British anti-slavery newspaper. "I had much rather starve in England, a free woman," she wrote, "than be a slave for the best man that ever breathed upon the American continent."

The next selections deal with slaves who turned themselves into cargo; of the two, the better-known is Henry "Box" Brown. "A man of invention as well as a hero" — as William Still, the principal conductor in the Philadelphia underground railroad, put it — this Richmond, Virginia, slave had himself crated up in a box two feet, eight inches deep, two feet wide, and three feet long, and forwarded to Philadelphia by express. With only "one bladder [skin-canteen] of water and a few small biscuits to sustain him," Brown endured a hazardous twenty-six-hour journey, sometimes riding upside down. Finally deposited in Philadelphia, the box was unpacked by abolitionists, who were pleased and surprised to see Brown emerge, hand extended, with the greeting, "How do you do, gentlemen." Brown later told his story to abolitionist audiences, utilizing his now famous box as a stage prop. The other slave who survived a box ride, this one from Baltimore to Philadelphia, was William Peel Jones. Again it is William Still, who wrote a 780-page compendium of the underground railway's activities, whose account of Jones's strange odyssey is reproduced here.

The following account of two escapes by deception we owe to William Wells Brown's novel, Clotel.

As a number of slaves revealed, leaving behind family could force the most difficult decision a runaway had to make. On a few recorded occasions, the successful fugitive returned to bring out someone he loved. The Delaware Anti-Slavery Association announced one such incident, the escape of John Moore with his wife.

If a slave was discouraged from attempting the long, perilous journey North and yet was still determined to flee, he might take to the woods, swamps, or hills. Or he might retreat to an underground existence in a cave. A former Georgia slave woman, reminiscing in the 1930's about her past, told of one such case; her account completes this segment.

The Thoughts of Rev. J. W. C. Pennington*

It is impossible for me now to recollect all the perplexing thoughts that passed through my mind during that fornoon; it was a day of heartaching to me. But I distinctly remember the two great difficulties

***

* From William Loren Katz, ed., *Five Slave Narratives: a Compendium*, vol. 2 (New York, 1968), pp. 12–14. Punctuation slightly changed.

that stood in the way of my flight: I had a father and mother whom I dearly loved, I had also six sisters and four brothers on the plantation. The question was, shall I hide my purpose from them? Moreover, how will my flight affect them when I am gone? Will they not be suspected? Will not the whole family be sold off as a disaffected family, as is generally the case when one of its members flies? But a still more trying question was, how can I expect to succeed, I have no knowledge of distance or direction—I know that Pennsylvania is a free state, but I know not where its soil begins, or where that of Maryland ends? Indeed, at this time there was no safety in Pennsylvania, New Jersey, or New York, for a fugitive except in lurking-places, or under the care of judicious friends, who could be entrusted not only with liberty, but with life itself.

With such difficulties before my mind, the day had rapidly worn away; and it was just past noon. One of my perplexing questions I had settled—I had resolved to let no one into my secret; but the other difficulty was now to be met. It was to be met without the least knowledge of its magnitude, except by imagination. Yet of one thing there could be no mistake, that the consequences of a failure would be most serious. Within my recollection no one had attempted to escape from my master; but I had many cases in my mind's eye of slaves of other planters who had failed, and who had been made examples of the most cruel treatment by flogging and selling to the far South where they were never to see their friends more. I was not without serious apprehension that such would be my fate. The bare possibility was impressively solemn; but the hour was now come, and the man must act and be free or remain a slave for ever. How the impression came to be upon my mind I cannot tell; but there was a strange and horrifying belief that if I did not meet the crisis that day I should be self-doomed—that my ear would be nailed to the door-post for ever. The emotions of that moment I cannot fully depict—hope, fear, dread, terror, love, sorrow, and deep melancholy were mingled in my mind together; my mental state was one of most painful distraction. When I looked at my numerous family—a beloved father and mother, eleven brothers and sisters, etc.; but when I looked at slavery as such; when I looked at it in its mildest form, with all its annoyances; and above all, when I remembered that one of the chief annoyances of slavery in the most mild form is the liability of being at any moment sold into the worst form; it seemed that no consideration, not even that of life itself, could tempt me to give up the thought of flight. And then when I considered the difficulties of the way—the reward that would be offered—the human blood-hounds that would be set upon my track—the weariness—

the hunger—the gloomy thought of not only losing all one's friends in one day, but of having to seek and to make new friends in a strange world. But, as I have said, the hour was come, and the man must act, or for ever be a slave.

Henry Bibb's Experiences*

Among other good trades I learned the art of running away to perfection. I made a regular business of it, and never gave it up, until I had broken the bands of slavery, and landed myself safely in Canada, where I was regarded as a man, and not as a thing.

The first time in my life that I ran away was for ill treatment, in 1825. I was living with a Mr. Vires, in the village of Newcastle. His wife was a very cross woman. She was every day flogging me, boxing, pulling my ears, and scolding, so that I dreaded to enter the room where she was. This first started me to running away from them. I was often gone several days before I was caught. They would abuse me for going off, but it did no good. The next time they flogged me, I was off again; but after awhile they got sick of their bargain, and returned me back into the hands of my owners. By this time Mr. White had married his second wife. She was what I call a tyrant. I lived with her several months, but she kept me almost half of my time in the woods, running from under the bloody lash. While I was at home she kept me all the time rubbing furniture, washing, scrubbing the floors; and when I was not doing this, she would often seat herself in a large rocking chair, with two pillows about her, and would make me rock her, and keep off the flies. She was too lazy to scratch her own head, and would often make me scratch and comb it for her. She would at other times lie on her bed, in warm weather, and make me fan her while she slept, scratch and rub her feet; but after awhile she got sick of me, and preferred a maiden servant to do such business. I was then hired out again; but by this time I had become much better skilled in running away, and would make calculation to avoid detection, by taking with me a bridle. If any body should see me in the woods, as they have, and asked "what are doing here sir? you are a runaway?"— I said, "no, sir, I am looking for our old mare"; at other times, "looking for our cows." For such excuses I was let pass. In fact, the only weapon of self-defence that I could use successfully was that of de-

---

* Henry Bibb, *Narrative of the Life and Adventures of Henry Bibb, an American Slave* (New York, 1849), pp. 15-17, 47.

ception. It is useless for a poor helpless slave to resist a white man in a slaveholding State. Public opinion and the law is against him; and resistance in many cases is death to the slave, while the law declares that he shall submit or die.

.   .   .   .

Every inducement was held out to me to run away if I would be free, and the voice of liberty was thundering in my very soul, "Be free, oh, man! be free"; I was struggling against a thousand obstacles which had clustered around my mind to bind my wounded spirit still in the dark prison of mental degradation. My strong attachments to friends and relatives, with all the love of home and birth-place which is so natural among the human family, twined about my heart and were hard to break away from. And withal, the fear of being pursued with guns and blood-hounds, and of being killed, or captured and taken to the extreme South, to linger out my days in hopeless bondage on some cotton or sugar plantation, all combined to deter me. But I had counted the cost, and was fully prepared to make the sacrifice. The time for fulfilling my pledge was then at hand. I must forsake friends and neighbors, wife and child, or consent to live and die a slave.

The Escape of William and Ellen Craft*

William and Ellen Craft, man and wife, lived with different masters in the state of Georgia. Ellen is so near white that she can pass without suspicion for a white woman. Her husband is much darker. He is a mechanic, and by working nights and Sundays he laid up money enough to bring himself and his wife out of slavery. Their plan was without precedent, and though novel, was the means of getting them their freedom. Ellen dressed in man's clothing, and passed as the *master*, while her husband passed as the *servant*. In this way they travelled from Georgia to Philadelphia. They are now out of the reach of the bloodhounds of the South. On their journey, they put up at the best hotels where they stopped. Neither of them can read or write. And Ellen, knowing that she would be called upon to write her name at the hotels, etc., tied her right hand up as though it was lame, which proved of some service to her as she was called upon several times at hotels to "register" her name. In Charleston, S. C., they put up at the hotel which Governor M'Duffie and John C. Calhoun generally

---

* From an article by William Wells Brown in *The Liberator* (January 12, 1849). Punctuation altered.

make their home, yet these distinguished advocates of the "peculiar institution" say that the slaves cannot take care of themselves. They arrived in Philadelphia in four days from the time they started. Their history, especially that of their escape, is replete with interest. They will be at the meeting of the Massachusetts Anti-Slavery Society, in Boston, in the latter part of this month, where I know the history of their escape will be listened to with great interest. They are very intelligent. They are young, Ellen 22, and William 25 years of age. Ellen is truly a heroine.

William Peel Jones in a Box*

William is twenty-five years of age, unmistakably colored, good-looking, rather under the medium size, and of pleasing manners. William had himself boxed by a near relative and forwarded by the Erricson line of steamers. He gave the slip to Robert H. Carr, his owner (a grocer and commission merchant), after this wise and for the following reasons: for some time previous his master had been selling off his slaves every now and then, the same as other groceries, and this admonished William that he was liable to be in the market any day; consequently, he preferred the box to the auction-block.

He did not complain of having been treated very badly by Carr, but felt that no man was safe while owned by another. In fact, he "hated the very name of slaveholder." The limit of the box not admitting of straightening himself out he was taken with the cramp on the road, suffered indescribable misery, and had his faith taxed to the utmost—indeed was brought to the very verge of "screaming aloud" ere relief came. However, he controlled himself, though only for a short season, for before a great while an excessive faintness came over him. Here nature became quite exhausted. He thought he must "die"; but his time had not yet come. After a severe struggle he revived, but only to encounter a third ordeal no less painful than the one through which he had just passed. Next a very "cold chill" came over him, which seemed almost to freeze the very blood in his veins and gave him intense agony, from which he only found relief on awaking, having actually fallen asleep in that condition. Finally, however, he arrived at Philadelphia, on a steamer, Sabbath morning. A devoted friend of his, expecting him, engaged a carriage and repaired to the wharf for the box. The bill of lading and the receipt he had with him, and like-

---

* Reprinted from William Still, *Underground Rail Road Records* (Philadelphia, 1883), pp. 46–48, with slight changes in punctuation.

wise knew where the box was located on the boat. Although he well knew freight was not usually delivered on Sunday, yet his deep solicitude for the safety of his friend determined him to do all that lay in his power to rescue him from his perilous situation. Handing his bill of lading to the proper officer of the boat, he asked if he could get the freight that it called for. The officer looked at the bill and said, "No, we do not deliver freight on Sunday," but, noticing the anxiety of the man, he asked him if he would know it if he were to see it. Slowly—fearing that too much interest manifested might excite suspicion—he replied: "I think I should." Deliberately looking around amongst all the "freight," he discovered the box, and said, "I think that is it there." Said officer stepped to it, looked at the directions on it, then at the bill of lading, and said, "That is right, take it along." Here the interest in these two bosoms was thrilling in the highest degree. But the size of the box was too large for the carriage, and the driver refused to take it. Nearly an hour and a half was spent in looking for a furniture car. Finally one was procured, and again the box was laid hold of by the occupant's particular friend, when, to his dread alarm, the poor fellow within gave a sudden cough. At this startling circumstance he dropped the box; equally as quick, although dreadfully frightened, and, as if helped by some invisible agency, he commenced singing, "Hush, my babe, lie still and slumber," with the most apparent indifference, at the same time slowly making his way from the box. Soon his fears subsided, and it was presumed that no one was any the wiser on account of the accident, or coughing. Thus, after summoning courage, he laid hold of the box a third time, and the Rubicon was passed. The car driver, totally ignorant of the contents of the box, drove to the number to which he was directed to take it—left it and went about his business. Now is a moment of intense interest—now of inexpressible delight. The box is opened, the straw removed, and the poor fellow is loosed and is rejoicing, I will venture to say, as mortal never did rejoice, who had not been in similar peril. This particular friend was scarcely less overjoyed, however, and their joy did not abate for several hours; nor was it confined to themselves, for two invited members of the Vigilance Committee also partook of a full share. The box man was named Wm. Jones. He was boxed up in Baltimore by the friend who received him at the wharf, who did not come in the boat with him, but came in the cars and met him at the wharf.

The trial in the box lasted just seventeen hours before victory was achieved. Jones was well cared for by the Vigilance Committee and sent on his way rejoicing, feeling that Resolution, Underground Rail Road, and Liberty were invaluable.

Two Stories by William Wells Brown*

A slave was one day seen passing on the high road from a border town in the interior of the state of Virginia to the Ohio river. The man had neither hat upon his head or coat upon his back. He was driving a very nice fat pig, and appeared to all who saw him to be a labourer employed on an adjoining farm. *No negro is permitted to go at large in the Slave States without a written pass from his or her master, except on business in the neighborhood.* "Where do you live, my boy?" asked a white man of the slave, as he passed a white house with green blinds. "Just up de road, sir," was the answer. "That's a fine pig." "Yes, sir, marser like dis shoat berry much." And this way he and the pig travelled more than fifty miles before they reached the Ohio river. Once at the river they crossed over; the pig was sold; and nine days after the runaway slave passed over the Niagara river, and, for the first time in his life, breathed the air of freedom.

A few weeks later and on the same road, two slaves were seen passing; one was on horseback, the other was walking before him with his arms tightly bound, and a long rope leading from the man on foot to the one on horseback. "Oh, ho, that's a runaway rascal, I suppose," said a farmer, who met them on the road. "Yes sir, he bin runaway, and I got him fast. Marser will tan his jacket for him nicely when he gets him." "You are a trustworthy fellow, I imagine," continued the farmer. "Oh yes, sir; marser puts a heap of confidence in dis nigger." And the slaves travelled on. When the one on foot was fatigued, they would change positions. This they called "ride and tie." After a journey of more than two hundred miles they reached the Ohio river, turned the horse loose, told him to go home, and proceeded on their way to Canada.

John Moore Returns for His Wife†

Just from Slavery—John Moore and wife with two others have just arrived safely from Kentucky. Mr. Moore desires to be kindly remembered to Elijah Moore of Kentucky, his former owner, and [reports] that they had a very pleasant trip out, that his wife was in rather delicate health when they left Kentucky, but a change of atmosphere, coming where it is unpolluted with slavery, has greatly improved her.

---

* From Brown's novel, *Clotel* (Philadelphia, 1855), pp. 164–165; slight typographical changes.

† From the *National Anti-Slavery Standard* (June 19, 1851), with alterations in punctuation.

This is the second time Mr. Moore has run away for his freedom. In the summer of 1850 he fled into the state of Indiana, where he hired for the term of two months, and saved his wages. At the close of the term he returned to Kentucky with all his wages and handed all over to his master, declaring at the same time that he was sick of freedom and the abolitionists, he wanted a home that he could depend upon in sickness and at all times, that the abolitionists were not to be trusted, etc. This of course threw him right into the confidence of his master, and he was received back as a faithful slave. Many of his master's neighbors tried to make him sell him fearing that he had only come back to steal his wife who belonged to a neighboring plantation. But this master refused to sell him on the ground of his being so honest.

The man who owned his wife would not allow him to visit her for fear he would steal her off. But Mr. Moore pretended to care nothing about his wife, but would slip in and see her every night about midnight. Finally her master informed him that he might come and take his things off if he wanted them. So he went on Sunday and gathered up his bed, clothing, etc., and abused his wife like a dog so far as words go, and said he never wanted to speak to her again. This conduct removed all jealousy from her master's mind, and he would occasionally let her go out Sundays and nights without watching her. So she asked leave to go a-visiting on Saturday night with the privilege of staying until Sunday evening, which was granted, and her husband took her that night and never stopped short of Canada.

Hiding in a Cave*

One of the slaves married a young gal, and they put her in the big house to work. One day Mistress jumped on her 'bout something, and the gal hit her back; Mistress said she was going to have Master put her in the stock and beat her when he come home. When the gal went to the field and told her husband 'bout it, he told her where to go and stay till he got there. That night he took his supper to her. He carried her to a cave and hauled pine straw and put in there for her to sleep on. He fixed that cave up just like a house for her, put a stove in there and run a pipe out through the ground into a swamp. Everybody always wondered how he fixed that pipe. Course they didn't cook on it till night when nobody could see the smoke. He ceiled the house

* B. A. Botkin, ed. *Lay My Burden Down: A Folk History of Slavery* (Chicago, 1965), pp. 179–180.

with pine logs, made beds and tables out of pine poles, and they lived in this cave seven years. During this time, they had three children. Nobody was with her when these children was born but her husband. He waited on her with each child. The children didn't wear no clothes 'cept a piece tied round their waists. They was just as hairy as wild people, and they was wild. When they come out of that cave, they would run every time they seed a person.

The seven years she lived in the cave, different folks helped 'em in food. Her husband would take it to a certain place and she would go and git it. People had passed over this cave ever so many times, but nobody knowed these folks was living there. Our master didn't know where she was, and it was freedom 'fore she come out of that cave for good.

SECTION 2.   DECEPTION

Irritated by the popular view held by Southerners and many Northerners that the slave enjoyed his way of life, Benjamin Drew, a white Boston school principal and part-time journalist, traveled to Canada where he interviewed more than one hundred ex-slaves concerning their thoughts and feelings about slavery. In 1855 his findings were published in *A North-Side View of Slavery*, which has become our best single source on slavery from the slave perspective. A particularly incisive commentary was obtained from John Little, a prospering farm owner of Queen's Bush in upper Canada (present-day Ontario). Little told Drew: " 'Tisn't he who has stood and looked on, that can tell you what slavery is — 'tis he who has endured." Wearing a happy appearance, he further explained, enabled a slave to cope with wretched reality. Some other remarks of Little's make up the next selection.

In the 1930's the Federal Writer's Project under the New Deal collected more than two thousand depositions in eighteen states from persons then in their seventies and eighties (and some even older) who had lived under Southern slavery. The best of these were edited by B. A. Botkin, a folklorist, and published under the title, *Lay My Burden Down*. In the second document reprinted in this section, Mrs. Josie Jordan, 75, a former Tennessee slave, recalls how a group of wily slaves, at the expense of their plantation master, got both physical and psychological nourishment.

Sometimes the rewards of deception were less tangible than in Mrs. Jordan's account, resting mainly in the befuddlement or irritation of the master, but often enough they involved a lightening of the slaves' tasks. Acknowledging no obligation to a system that exploited them only for their laboring abilities, many slaves did as little work as possible. They became accomplished at finding ways to get out of work or to slow it down considerably, often by becoming conveniently irresponsible or stubborn. The success of one such maneuver was unknowingly recorded by Charles Lyell, the famous English geologist, who was sufficiently irritated by the incident to remember to include it in his book of North American traveling experiences. The episode is called here "The Lost Glove."

Sabotage was a common sort of resistance among slaves. In some instances it might take a form as inconsequential — but as revealing — as that described in the autobiographical account by William Wells Brown, wherein he tells of his childhood experience with a bottle of his master's wine. The cruel treatment of stock animals and the destruction of farm tools were types of sabotage often mentioned in accounts of slavery. In such ways slaves' aggressive feelings toward the owner were directed against his possessions, at the same time hurting him economically. A selection from Frederick Law Olmsted's *Journey in the Seaboard Slave States* (1856) describes the results of such violent actions.

The next two documents are also from the narrative of Olmsted, a strong critic of slavery and discerning writer for the *New York Daily Times*. One discusses the common practice of temporary escape into a forest or swamp — the only vacation available to most slaves — and the other an analogous practice, that of feigning illness. The final selection in this section, from the writings of J. S. Buckingham (an English anti-slavery sympathizer), relates further instances of spurious sickness.

John Little — Dancing in Chains*

How can men who know they are abusing others all the day lie down and sleep quietly at night, with big barns of corn, and gin-houses full of cotton, when they know that men feel revengeful and might burn their property or even kill them? Even now the thought of my cruel abuses begins sometimes to creep up and kindle my feelings until I

---

* From Benjamin Drew, *The Refugee: a North-Side View of Slavery*, with an introduction by Tilden G. Edelstein (Redding, Massachusetts, 1969), pp. 156–157; punctuation altered.

feel unhappy in my own house, and it seems as if the devil was getting the better of me; I feel, then, that I could destroy that tyrant who, knowing that I was a man, cut me with a whip in a manner worse than I will name. Then I think, "What is the use? Here I am, a free man in Canada and out of his power." Yet I feel the stirrings of revenge. I know that thousands in the South feel the same, for we have counselled upon it; the slaveholders know this—how will they sleep nights? The slaveholder is afraid of his slaves: it cannot be otherwise. Some have been round the borders of slavery and seen a little of the edges of it, and they think they know a great deal about it, but they are mistaken. I have been in slavery, and know its worst is hid from them. They have all the laws and customs of the country in their favor, and yet they find something to grumble about; how then can they expect [that] the slaves, whose feelings are wretched even when they are best-used, can be happy and contented? They say the slaves are happy because they laugh and are merry. I myself, and three or four others, have received two hundred lashes in the day and had our feet in fetters: yet, at night we would sing and dance, and make others laugh at the rattling of our chains. Happy men we must have been! We did it to keep down trouble, and to keep our hearts from being completely broken: that is as true as gospel! Just look at it—consider upon it— must not we have been very happy? Yet I have done it myself—I have cut capers in chains!

A Case of Malitis*

I remember Mammy told me about one master who almost starved his slaves. Mighty stingy, I reckon he was.

Some of them slaves was so poorly thin they ribs would kinda rustle against each other like corn stalks a-drying in the hot winds. But they gets even one hog-killing time, and it was funny, too, Mammy said.

They was seven hogs, fat and ready for fall hog-killing time. Just the day before Old Master told off they was to be killed, something happened to all them porkers. One of the field boys found them and come a-telling the master: "The hogs is all died, now they won't be any meats for the winter."

When the master gets to where at the hogs is laying, they's a lot of Negroes standing round looking sorrow-eyed at the wasted meat. The master asks: "What's the illness with 'em?"

* From the account of Mrs. Josie Jordan in B. A. Botkin, ed., *Lay My Burden Down: A Folk History of Slavery* (Chicago, 1965), pp. 4–5.

"Malitis," they tells him, and they acts like they don't want to touch the hogs. Master says to dress them anyway for they ain't no more meat on the place.

He says to keep all the meat for the slave families, but that's because he's afraid to eat it hisself account of the hogs' got malitis.

"Don't you all know what is malitis?" Mammy would ask the children when she was telling of the seven fat hogs and seventy lean slaves. And she would laugh, remembering how they fooled Old Master so's to get all them good meats.

"One of the strongest Negroes got up early in the morning," Mammy would explain, "long 'fore the rising horn called the slaves from their cabins. He skitted to the hog pen with a heavy mallet in his hand. When he tapped Mister Hog 'tween the eyes with that mallet, 'malitis' set in might quick, but it was a uncommon 'disease,' even with hungry Negroes around all the time."

The Lost Glove*

On another occasion we were proceeding in a well-appointed carriage with a planter, when we came unexpectedly to a dead halt. Inquiring the cause, the black coachman said he had dropped one of his white gloves on the road, and must drive back and try to find it. He could not recollect within a mile where he had last seen it: we remonstrated, but in vain. As time pressed, the master in despair took off his own gloves, and, saying he had a second pair, gave them to him. When our charioteer had deliberately put them on, we started again.

William Wells Brown Refills a Wine Bottle†

Being sent one Sabbath morning to carry the sacramental wine to the church about a mile distant, I could not withstand the temptation it presented of tasting it. Having had one swallow, I was tempted further on till the beverage disappeared out of the neck of the bottle, so that I felt afraid that if noticed by master I should be flogged. It occurred to me that I might fill up the bottle frome one of the sap tubes, as I passed through the sugar camp; for it was the spring of the year, and we were making maple sugar. I tried to pour the sap into the bottle, but it flared over the top, leaving the wine still some

* Charles Lyell, *Travels in North America with Geological Observations on the United States, Canada and Nova Scotia*, vol. 1 (London, 1845), pp. 169-170.

† William Wells Brown, *The Black Man, His Antecedents, His Genius, and Achievements* (New York, 1863), p. 18; reprinted with changes in punctuation.

inches down the neck. After ransacking my inventive faculties, I fortunately hit upon a plan and filled it up. Placing the bottle on the ground, and sucking my mouth full of juice, I stood directly over the bottle and let it stream in until it was full. Putting the stopple in, I started off towards the church, feeling that I had got the advantage of master once more.

Plantation Sabotage*

I am shown tools that no man in his senses, with us [Northerners], would allow a laborer to whom he was paying wages to be encumbered with; and the excessive weight and clumsiness of which, I would judge, would make work at least ten percent greater than those ordinarily used with us. And I am assured that, in the careless and clumsy way they must be used by the slaves, anything lighter or less rude could not be furnished them with good economy, and that such tools as we constantly give our laborers, and find our profit in giving them, would not last out a day in a Virginia corn-field—much lighter and more free from stones though it be than ours.

So, too, when I ask why mules are so universally substituted for horses on the farm, the first reason given, and confessedly the most conclusive one, is that horses cannot bear the treatment that they always *must* get from negroes; horses are always soon foundered or crippled by them, while mules will bear cudgeling and lose a meal or two now and then and not be materially injured, and they do not take cold or get sick if neglected or overworked. But I do not need to go further than to the window of the room in which I am writing to see, at almost any time, treatment of cattle that would insure the immediate discharge of the driver by almost any farmer owning them at the North.

Vacation in the Swamp

The slave, if he is indisposed to work, and especially if he is not treated well or does not like the master who has hired him, will sham sickness—even make himself sick or lame—that he need not work. But a more serious loss frequently arises when the slave, thinking he is worked too hard or being angered by punishment or unkind treatment,

---

* This selection and the next two are reprinted with minor typographical changes from Frederick Law Olmsted, *A Journey in the Seaboard Slave States* (New York, 1856), pp. 46–47, 100–101, 187–190.

"getting the sulks" takes to "the swamp" and comes back when he has a mind to. Often this will not be till the year is up for which he is engaged, when he will return to his owner, who, glad to find his property safe, and that it has not died in the swamp or gone to Canada, forgets to punish him and immediately sends him for another year to a new master.

"But, meanwhile, how does the negro support life in the swamp?" I asked.

"Oh, he gets sheep and pigs and calves, and fowls and turkeys; sometimes they will kill a small cow. We have often seen the fires where they were cooking them, through the woods in the swamp yonder. If it is cold, he will crawl under a fodderstack, or go into the cabins with some of the other negroes, and in the same way, you see, he can get all the corn or almost anything else he wants.

"He steals them from his master?"

"From any one; frequently from me. I have had many a sheep taken by them."

"It is a common thing, then?"

"Certainly it is very common, and the loss is sometimes exceedingly provoking. One of my neighbors here was going to build, and hired two mechanics for a year. Just as he was ready to put his house up, the two men, taking offense at something, both ran away and did not come back at all till their year was out, and then their owner immediately hired them out again to another man."

These negroes "in the swamp," he said, were often hunted after, but it was very difficult to find them, and if caught they would run again and the other negroes would hide and assist them. Dogs to track them he had never known to be used in Virginia.

Suspicious Illnesses

I have never made the inquiry on any plantation where as many as twenty negroes were employed together that I have not ascertained that one or more of the field hands was not at work on account of some illness, strain, bruise, or wound of which he or she was complaining; and in such cases I have hardly ever heard the proprietor or overseer fail to express his suspicion that the invalid was really as well able to work as any one else on the plantation. It is said to be nearly as difficult to form a satisfactory diagnosis of negroes' disorders as it is of infants', because their imagination of symptoms is so vivid and because not the smallest reliance is to be placed on their accounts of what they have felt or done. If a man is really ill he fears lest he should be thought to be simulating, and therefore exaggerates all his pains and locates them in whatever he supposes to be the most vital parts of his system.

Frequently the invalid slaves will neglect or refuse to use the remedies prescribed for their recovery. They will conceal pills, for instance, under their tongue and declare they have swallowed them, when, from their producing no effect, it will be afterwards evident that they have not. This general custom I heard ascribed to habit, acquired when they were not very disagreeably ill and were loth to be made quite well enough to have to go to work again.

Amusing incidents illustrating this difficulty I have heard narrated, showing that the slave rather enjoys getting a severe wound that lays him up:—he has his hand crushed by the fall of a piece of timber, and after the pain is alleviated, is heard to exclaim, "Bress der Lord—der haan b'long to masser—don't reckon dis chile got no more corn to hoe dis yaar, no how." . . .

. . . The liability of women, especially, to disorders and irregularities which cannot be detected by exterior symptoms, but which may be easily aggravated into serious complaints, renders many of them nearly valueless for work because of the ease with which they can impose upon their owners. "The women on a plantation," said one extensive Virginian slave-owner to me, "will hardly earn their salt after they come to the breeding age: they don't come to the field, and you go to the quarters and ask the old nurse what's the matter, and she says, 'Oh, she's not well, master; she's not fit to work, sir,' and what can you do? You have to take her word for it that something or other is the matter with her, and you dare not set her to work; and so she lays up till she feels like taking the air again, and plays the lady at your expense."

I was on one plantation where a woman had been excused from any sort of labor for more than two years on the supposition that she was dying of phthisis [tuberculosis]. At last the overseer discovered that she was employed as a milliner and dress-maker by all the other colored ladies of the vicinity, and upon taking her to the house it was found that she had acquired a remarkable skill in these vocations. She was hired out the next year to a fashionable dress-maker in town at handsome wages; and as after that she did not again "raise blood," it was supposed that when she had done so before it had been by artificial means. Such tricks every army and navy surgeon is familiar with.

Ways of Feigning Sickness*

It is usual here also to say that, supposing the slaves were made free, they would be unable to maintain themselves and would not work even for their own benefit, as they are incapable of voluntary exertion. Yet in the face of this often-repeated assertion, I learnt here the following facts, and from the same persons that so confidently insisted on the indolence and incapacity of the slaves.

A wealthy planter said to me, "I assure you that these negroes are the laziest creatures in the world, and would never work but by compulsion. Now I have a fellow on my plantation, who for fourteen or fifteen days past has been complaining of rheumatism, and could not be brought to work for an hour; he was so ill, as he said, as to be unable. On Sunday last I was walking on the bay, looking down the river, when who should I see but my rheumatic rascal pulling up in his boat with some things to sell on his own account, the fellow having rowed a distance of fourteen or fifteen miles for a market." I replied, "The reason is very plain: he was too ill to work for *you* because he got nothing more by working than by being idle; but he was quite well enough to work for *himself* because his labour was well rewarded." "Egad!" said the planter, "but you have hit it; that is no doubt the cause of the difference."

. . . .

This same gentleman [not the one in the previous passage] told us of two instances that had happened on his own estate, of ingenious evasions of labour. One man took medicine which he stole from the dispensary purposely to make himself sick, to avoid work, and when examined by the doctor he was detected in having spread powdered mustard on his tongue to give it a foul appearance. A female slave, to avoid working for her master, produced such swellings in her arms as to excite the compassion of those who thought it to be some dreadful disease; but the same person, who lay abed groaning with agony all day, being detected in the act of washing clothes at night for some persons in the neighbourhood, for which she was to be paid—and to effect which in secrecy she was found standing nearly up to her middle in a pond concealed under the trees—afterwards confessed, in order to avoid a flogging, that she had produced the swelling in her arms by thrusting them into a beehive and keeping them there till they were thoroughly bitten and stung; and when the swelling began to subside, she repeated the same operation to revive them.

* From J. S. Buckingham, *The Slave States of America*, vol. 1 (London, 1842), pp. 135, 402. Punctuation slightly changed.

SECTION 3. VIOLENCE AGAINST SELF

Some slaves carried their resistance to the frantic extremes of self violence and, beyond that, suicide. A beating, harsh words, sale of a loved one — any number of incidents might provoke a slave into an act of injury to himself. Ex-slave Charles Ball remarked that "self-destruction is much more frequent among slaves in the cotton region than is generally supposed. When a Negro kills himself, the master is unwilling to let it be known. . . . Suicide amongst the slaves is regarded as a matter of dangerous example, and one which it is the business and the interest of all proprietors to discountenance, and prevent." The documents that follow illustrate several of the ways in which slaves brought injury or death to themselves and at least monetary loss to their owners.

Revenge for an Injustice*

The personal oppression of the negroes is the grossest vice which strikes a stranger in the country. It can never be otherwise when human beings are wholly subjected to the will of other human beings who are under no other external control than the law which forbids killing and maiming—a law which it is difficult to enforce in individual cases. A fine slave was walking about in Columbia, South Carolina, when I was there, nearly helpless and useless from the following causes. His master was fond of him, and the slave enjoyed the rare distinction of never having been flogged. One day, his master's child, supposed to be under his care at the time, fell down and hurt itself. The master flew into a passion, ordered the slave to be instantly flogged, and would not hear a single word the man had to say. As soon as the flogging was over, the slave went into the back yard, where there was an axe and a block, and struck off the upper half of his right hand. He went and held up the bleeding hand before his master, saying, "You have mortified me, so I have made myself useless. Now you must maintain me as long as I live." It came out that the child had been under the charge of another person.

---

* From Harriet Martineau, *Society in America*, vol. 2 (New York, 1837), pp. 112–113; typographical alterations.

Spite*

I have to-day in company with an estimable German gentleman resident at Richmond, visited some of the negro jails, that is those places of imprisonment in which negroes are in part punished and in part confined for sale. I saw in one of these jails a tall, strong-limbed negro, sitting silent and gloomy, with his right hand wrapped in a cloth. I asked if he were ill.

"No," replied his loquacious keeper, "but he is a very bad rascal. His master, who lives up the river, has parted him from his wife and children, to sell him down South as he wanted to punish him, and now the scoundrel, to be revenged upon his master and to make himself fetch a less sum of money, has cut off the fingers of his right hand! The rascal asked me to lend him an ax to knock the nails into his shoes with, and I lent it him without suspecting any bad intention, and now has the fellow gone and maimed himself for life!"

Death Was Far Preferable†

When we had passed a few miles out of Albany, the boat hove to and there came on board four men—one of the number a colored man. The white men repaired to their staterooms, leaving the colored man on deck, after the boat had returned to the channel. He attracted my attention, by his dejected appearance and apparent hopeless despair. He was, I judged, about forty years of age; his clothing coarse and very ragged; and the most friendless, sorrowful-looking being I ever saw. He spake to no one, but silently paced the deck—his breast heaving with inaudible sighs, his brow contracted with a most terrible frown, his eyes dreamily fastened on the floor—and he appeared to be considering on some hopeless undertaking. I watched him attentively as I walked to and fro on the same deck, and could clearly discover that some fearful conflict was taking place in his mind; but as I afterwards repassed him he looked up with a happy, patient smile that lighted up his whole countenance, which seemed to say plainly: I see

---

* Reprinted with changes in punctuation from Fredrika Bremer, *Homes of the New World: Impressions of America*, vol. 2 (New York, 1853), p. 533.

† From *Austin Steward: Twenty-Two Years a Slave and Forty Years a Freeman*, with an introduction by Jane H. and William H. Pease (Redding, Mass., 1969), pp. 150–151; changes in punctuation.

a way of escape and have decided on my course of action. His whole appearance was changed; his heart that before had beat so wildly was quiet now as the broad bosom of the Hudson, and he gazed after me with a look of calm deliberation, indicative of a settled but desperate purpose. I walked hastily forward and turned around, when, Oh, my God! what a sight was there! Holding still the dripping knife, with which he had cut his throat! and while his life-blood oozed from the gaping wound and flowed over his tattered garments to the deck, the same exultant smile beamed on his ghastly features!

The history of the poor, dejected creature was now revealed: he had escaped from his cruel taskmaster in Maryland; but in the midst of his security and delightful enjoyment, he had been overtaken by the human bloodhound and returned to his avaricious and tyrannical master, now conducting him back to a life of Slavery, to which he rightly thought death was far preferable.

Bunch v. *Smith**

Bunch had agreed with Smith to sell him Bob, Binah, and her two children, for $1,100.

> [Smith] stepped up to Bob, and asked Bob how he would like him for a master. Bob said he would not suit. Smith replied, "I have not come to consult you; I have bought you; and if you run away from January to January, you are mine," and advised Bob to reconcile himself to the change and give him no further trouble. Soon after, Bob, having finished a job at which he was engaged, got up and was walking towards his house, when Smith advanced to him and said ... "it is of no use for you to run, for I have my dogs and can catch you." Bob replied that he would run from no man. Smith spoke a word of encouragement to him. Bob went to the negro house; Smith waited awhile, until the cart came. He then ordered Binah to go and get ready; that he wanted her master, while they were there, to deliver them to him. She went to the negro house; Bob was standing at the door; Smith ordered Bob to go and get ready. He walked off as if going round the house; Smith called to him, and he went into the house. Smith, Bunch, and Gilmore were standing near the door, when Bob came

---

* *Bunch* v. *Smith*, 4 Richardson 581–584, May 1851, in Helen Tunicliff Catterall, *Judicial Cases Concerning American Slavery and the Negro*, vol. 2 (Washington, 1936), pp. 425–426; typographical changes.

out ... with his throat cut, and bleeding; he made a few turns in the yard, fell on his knees, sank to the ground, and there bled to death. When he came out, Smith told Bunch he had better get the doctor. After the negro was dead, Smith said to Bunch it was no trade; to give to him, Smith, his notes [paper money] and he would give back to Bunch his bill of sale, and drew the bill of sale from his pocket. Bunch hesitated and said he was not aware whose loss it should be. Smith said to Bunch, it is your loss; the negroes were not delivered. ... A new trade was made for Binah and her two children for $650. ... There was some evidence that Bunch was of a temperament to be agitated by the shocking spectacle of Bob's death. ... It was submitted to the jury to determine whether Bob ... had been delivered ... before Bob's death. ... The jury found a verdict for the plaintiff for $450, with interest.

Motions in arrest of judgment, for non-suit, and for new trial, dismissed.

SECTION 4. VIOLENCE AGAINST WHITES

What the master viewed as stealing and the slave called "taking" was a regular feature of plantation life. It was tolerated up to a point by the owner, who excused it in part by theorizing that the black man was naturally incapable of distinguishing right from wrong. Contrarily, the owned, feeling that the master did not fairly distinguish between right and wrong, felt little if any guilt in acquiring for himself whatever of the master's food, clothing, and possessions were accessible. An English observer, J. S. Buckingham, who lost no opportunity to point out the tragedy of slavery to both indispensable parties, noted the prevalence of theft, especially at hotels, where attending slaves took advantage of every absence of white travelers from their rooms. Shortly out of Charleston, South Carolina, in 1839, Buckingham came upon a situation that both illustrates the role of theft in the slavery system and introduces a new subject for examination: overt destruction of white property and lives by slaves.

The following selection, also by Buckingham, recounts a case of arson. That slaves had the incendiary habit is obvious from the large number of fires reported in newspapers and court records. Methods of fire prevention were primitive and this, combined with the slaves' many chances for starting fires, was in part responsible for the curfew laws and night watches that characterized life after dark in the cities of the antebellum South. Of the two documents on arson, one is Buckingham's report of a hotel fire and the second is the court record of a barn-burning case.

For a slave to strike a white man meant almost certain punishment and, in some cases, death. Nevertheless, a number of ex-slaves told of fights with the masters or overseers. Frederick Douglass's account of his famous tumble with the slave-breaker Edward Covey is reprinted next in this section. Because Douglass had proved a difficult piece of property to handle, his master had turned him over to Covey, whose reputation as a tamer of slaves was well deserved. Covey, by Douglass's testimony, whipped him practically every week for six months. Then came a fateful day in August, 1833, when, as Douglass wrote of himself, "a slave was made a man."

A powerful symbol of the master's authority was the slave patrol, the principal police arm servicing the plantation community. Every Southern state, of necessity, had slave patrols, frequently made up of nonslaveholding whites who were drafted for the unpleasant duty; they were granted broad powers, such as the right to visit and search slave quarters and to break up unlawful slave assemblies. The patrollers — or "paddyrollers," or "paterollers" as they were variously called by the slaves — were particularly active in times of crisis. Slaves welcomed opportunities to defy them, as recalled by the elderly ex-slave whose 1830's reminiscences comprise the next selection.

"The abuse a man receives at the South," another ex-slave once explained, "is enough to drive every thing good from the mind. I sometimes felt such a spirit of vengeance, that I seriously meditated setting the house on fire at night, and killing all as they came out. I overcame the evil, and never got at it — but a little more punishment would have done it. I had been so bruised and wounded and beset, that I was out of patience." The public record indicates that many slaves, unable or unwilling to overcome the "evil," committed various acts of murder on the overseer or the master, and sometimes his whole family. Reports of four instances of murder conclude this section: first a short item from a Charleston newspaper about an alleged poisoning in 1738; then an Annapolis, Maryland, newspaper story of a slave woman who, on hearing that her master had provided for her freedom if he left no heirs, proceeded to poison his three children; next comes ex-slave Solomon Northup's report of a slave who chopped an overseer to death;

and finally, Charity Morris, also once a slave, tells about a black woman who murdered her master.

Cattle-Theft and Murder*

In the course of the afternoon we took in tow a longboat, rowed by twelve negroes, with a covered cabin in which were two slaves in custody of a white sheriff's officer, conveying them to one of the judicial stations for trial. It appeared that an overseer, or driver, on a plantation, had been shot dead by a negro belonging to an adjoining estate, and these two men were taken up on suspicion, one as the perpetrator and the other as an accomplice in the act. The reason assigned by our white informants on board for the murder was this: They alleged that the negroes were often in the habit of stealing cattle from their masters' plantations as well as from the neighbouring estates, and their overseer, being a vigilant man, had often detected them; so that to remove him, and thus carry on their depredations unmolested, they had shot him with a rifle. I inquired what they did with the stolen cattle when they escaped detection and was informed that they killed them in secret for food, some using the flesh themselves, others exchanging it with other negroes for rice; and some being given to runaway negroes, who were often secretly sustained in this manner by their fellow-slaves till they could get safely out of their hiding places and effect their escape.

A Burned Hotel

In the investigation which took place subsequently as to the cause of this fire, there was reason to believe that it was not accidental but the work of some of the slaves belonging to the establishment. The proprietor, Judge Hale, was a humane and kind master; but he resided in another house. . . . The manager and his assistants, being less just and considerate than the master, exercised, it was said, undue severity on the slaves or at least on some of them, and imprisonments and whippings were matters of frequent occurrence. In such cases it is a very usual mode of revenge with the slaves to burn down the houses

---

* This and the next selection, with typography somewhat altered, are from J. S. Buckingham, *The Slave States of America*, vol. 2 (London, 1842), pp. 86–87, and 50.

of their oppressors; for by this means they often succeed in breaking up an establishment in such a manner as to lead to a sale of their own persons; and then they have a chance of release from existing tyranny by being transferred to a new master, with a hope at least of better treatment.

Re Negro Beck*

"Conviction of Negro Beck. . . . Sentence of Death . . . for setting fire to and burning the Tobacco House and Tobacco . . . belonging to . . . Joseph Smith (her master). . . . The Consideration of this Matter is postponed until some further information can be had of her Character."
May 1766, letter from Charles Grahame, Esq.:

> . . . her youth and Confession of the Fact appearing to be the only Circumstances in her favour. . . . The negro drew some Cyder out of a Cask . . . and left it runing. . . . Her Mistress threatened to tell her Master and have her whipped. The Wench . . . applied several times to her Mistress begging forgiveness . . . and praying she would conceal it . . . but she refused. . . . The Negro went into the Kitchen, took a live Coal from the fire, carried it between two Chips to The Tobacco House, . . . and the Wind . . . blew up the Coal. . . . The Tobacco together with the House, the Dwelling House and some other Out-houses were entirely consumed. . . . Mrs. Smith came to my House and begged I would apply . . . for his Excellency's Pardon for the Wench, telling me if the Negro is Executed she can never forgive herself for obstinately Persisting in her Threat of having her punished . . . that she has heretofore behaved herself as well as negroes in Common do; Mr. Smith too is willing that His Excellency show her Mercy. . . . I must not Omitt to mention that there have been two other Tobacco Houses full of Tobacco burnt in this County this Winter. One of them . . . there is great Reason to Suspect was set on fire by her Negro Man Jack now in Prince George's County Gaol, he lately escaped out of the Prison of this County to which he had been committed for a Theft."

At the next meeting of the council, "Ordered . . . that Dead Warrant issue for the Execution of Negro Beck."

---

* Re Negro Beck, 32 Md Arch. 125–144, March 1766, from Helen Tunicliff Catterall, ed., Judicial Cases Concerning American Slavery and the Negro, vol. 4 (Washington, 1936), p. 45. Typography has been changed.

When Frederick Douglass Struck Back*

While I was obeying his order to feed and get the horses ready for the field, and when I was in the act of going up the stable-loft for the purpose of throwing down some blades, Covey sneaked into the stable in his peculiar way, and seizing me suddenly by the leg he brought me to the stable-floor, giving my newly-mended body a terrible jar. I now forgot all about my roots and remembered my pledge to stand up in my own defense. . . . I was resolved to fight, and what was better still I actually was hard at it. The fighting madness had come upon me and I found my strong fingers firmly attached to the throat of the tyrant, as heedless of consequences at the moment as if we stood as equals before the law. The very color of the man was forgotten. I felt supple as a cat and was ready for him at every turn. Every blow of his was parried, though I dealt no blows in return. I was strictly on the defensive, preventing him from injuring me rather than trying to injure him. I flung him on the ground several times when he meant to have hurled me there. I held him so firmly by the throat that his blood followed my nails. He held me, and I held him.

All was fair thus far, and the contest was about equal. My resistance was entirely unexpected and Covey was taken aback by it. He trembled in every limb. "Are you going to resist, you scoundrel?" said he. To which I returned a polite "Yes, sir," steadily gazing my interrogator in the eye, to meet the first approach or drawing of the blow which I expected my answer would call forth. But the conflict did not long remain equal. Covey soon cried lustily for help, not that I was obtaining any marked advantage over him or was injuring him, but because he was gaining none over me, and was not able, single-handed, to conquer me. He called for his cousin Hughes to come to his assistance, and now the scene was changed. I was compelled to give blows as well as to parry them, and since I was in any case to suffer for resistance, I felt (as the musty proverb goes) that I might as well be hanged for an old sheep as a lamb. I was still defensive toward Covey, but aggressive toward Hughes, on whom, at his first approach, I dealt a blow which fairly sickened him. He went off, bending over with pain, and manifesting no disposition to come again within my reach. . . .

Taken completely by surprise, Covey seemed to have lost his usual strength and coolness. He was frightened, and stood puffing and blowing, seemingly unable to command words or blows. When he saw that

---

* Frederick Douglass, *Life and Times of Frederick Douglass* (New York, 1962), 139–143. Reprinted with some changes in punctuation.

Hughes was standing half bent with pain, his courage quite gone, the cowardly tyrant asked if I meant to persist in my resistance. I told him I did mean to resist, come what might—that I had been treated like a brute during the last six months, and that I should stand it no longer. With that he gave me a shake, and attempted to drag me toward a stick of wood that was lying just outside the stable door. He meant to knock me down with it, but just as he leaned over to get the stick, I seized him with both hands by the collar, and with a vigorous and sudden snatch brought my assailant harmlessly his full length on the not over-clean ground, for we were now in the cowyard. He had selected the place for the fight and it was but right that he should have all the advantages of his own selection.

By this time Bill, the hired man, came home. He had been to Mr. Helmsley's to spend Sunday with his nominal wife. Covey and I had been skirmishing from before daybreak till now. . . . I could not see where the matter was to terminate. He evidently was afraid to let me go, lest I should again make off to the woods; otherwise he would probably have obtained arms from the house to frighten me. Holding me, he called upon Bill to assist him. The scene here had something comic about it. Bill, who knew precisely what Covey wished him to do, affected ignorance, and pretended he did not know what to do. "What shall I do, Master Covey?" said Bill. "Take hold of him! Take hold of him!" cried Covey. With a toss of his head, peculiar to Bill, he said: "Indeed, Master Covey, I want to go to work." "This is your work," said Covey, "take hold of him." Bill replied, with spirit, "My master hired me here to work, and not to help you whip Frederick." It was my turn to speak. "Bill," said I, "don't put your hands on me." To which he replied, "My God, Frederick, I ain't goin' to tech ye"; and Bill walked off, leaving Covey and myself to settle our differences as best we might.

But my present advantage was threatened when I saw Caroline (the slave woman of Covey) coming to the cowyard to milk, for she was a powerful woman, and could have mastered me easily, exhausted as I was.

As soon as she came near, Covey attempted to rally her to his aid. Strangely and fortunately, Caroline was in no humor to take a hand in any such sport. We were all in open rebellion that morning. Caroline answered the command of her master to "take hold of me," precisely as Bill had done, but in her it was at far greater peril, for she was the slave of Covey. . . .

At length (two hours had elapsed) the contest was given over. Letting go of me, puffing and blowing at a great rate, Covey said,

"Now, you scoundrel, go to your work; I would not have whipped you half so hard if you had not resisted." The fact was, he had not whipped me at all. He has not, in all the scuffle, drawn a single drop of blood from me. I had drawn blood from him, and should even without this satisfaction have been victorious, because my aim had not been to injure him but to prevent his injuring me.

During the whole six months that I lived with Covey after this transaction, he never again laid the weight of his finger on me in anger. He would occasionally say he did not want to have to get hold of me again—a declaration which I had no difficulty in believing—and I had a secret feeling which answered, "You had better not wish to get hold of me again, for you will likely to come off worse in a second fight than you did in the first."

This battle with Mr. Covey, undignified as it was and as I fear my narration of it is, was the turning-point in my "life as a slave." It rekindled in my breast the smouldering embers of liberty. It brought up Baltimore dreams and revived a sense of my own manhood. I was a changed being after that fight. I was nothing before—I was a man now. It recalled to life my crushed self-respect, and my self-confidence, and inspired me with a renewed determination to be a free man. A man without force is without the essential dignity of humanity. Human nature is so constituted that it cannot honor a helpless man, though it can pity him, and even this it cannot do long if signs of power do not arise.

Tripping Up the Paddyrollers*

... But there was ways of beating the patterollers. De best way was to head 'em off. I 'member once when we was gonna have a meetin' down in de woods near de river. Well, dey made me de lookout boy, an' when de paddyrollers come down de lane past de church—you see dey was 'spectin dat de niggers gonna hold a meetin' dat night—well, sir, dey tell me to step out f'm de woods an' let 'em see me. Well, I does, an' de paddyrollers dat was on horse back come a chasin' arter me, jus' a-gallopin' down de lane to beat de band. Well I was jus' ahead of 'em, an' when they got almost up wid me I jus' ducked into de woods. Course de paddyrollers couldn't stop so quick an' kep' on 'roun' de ben', an' den dere came a-screamin' an' cryin' dat make you think dat hell done bust loose. Dem old paddyrollers done rid plumb

* W.P.A. Federal Writers' Project, *The Negro in Virginia* (New York, 1940), p. 146.

into a great line of grape vines dat de slaves had stretched 'cross de path. An' dese vines tripped up de horses an' throwed de ole paddy-rollers off in de bushes. An' some done landed mighty hard, cause dey was a-limpin' roun' an' cussin' an' callin' fo' de slaves to come an' help dem, but dem slaves got plenty o' sense. Dey lay in de bushes an' hole dere sides a-laughin', but ain't none o' 'em gonna risk bein' seen. All right dat night, but de nex' mornin' gonna come. Help de white man den but in de mornin' he done forgot all 'bout how you help him. All he know is dat you was out. So after ole paddyrollers go on limpin' back to de town, we go on to de woods an' hold our meetin'.

A Poisoning Charge*

We have heard from Trenton, That two Negroes were last Week imprison'd on the following Occasion. 'Tis said that they were about to perswade another Negro to poison his Master; and to convince him of the Efficacy of the Drug which they presented him for that purpose, and the Security of giving it, let him know that Mr. Trent, and two of his Sons, Mr. Lambert and two of his Wives, and sundry other Persons were remov'd by their Slaves in that Manner. This Discourse being overheard, they were apprehended and 'tis said have made some Confession. But as the Persons above mentioned died apparently of common Distempers, it is not fully credited that any such Method was used to destroy them. The Drugs found on one of the Negroes were Arsenich and an unknown Kind of Root.

Quadruple Poisoning†

At the general court for the Eastern Shore now sitting, a negro woman, the property of Mr. Eccleston of Kent county in this state, was found guilty of the murder of the child of one of her fellow slaves, which she is said to have destroyed by means of laudanum. Humanity shudders at the guilt of this most atrocious wretch. She has, since her condemnation, acknowledged to have destroyed by poison three children of Robert Dunn, Esq., a most respectable and worthy gentleman of Kent. Her motive for this most horrid act appears to have been an expectation of being free if all the members of a particular family (the

---

* *South Carolina Gazette* (April 15, 1738).

† *Annapolis Gazette* (April 27, 1797) ; some changes in punctuation.

Bowers's), from whom she was [later] possessed [bought], were dead. She had been informed that a clause in the will of the late Mr. Bowers, of the same county, had destined his slaves to be free, if all his family should die! Let this serve as a solemn warning to those who are disposed to testamentary liberation of their slaves! The story of this dreadful affair is truly shocking.

The unhappy parents, returning from the funeral of their first child, found the second dead! and by the time they had paid the last offices to the second, the third expired! What pen—what eloquence can describe the condition of the unhappy parents! The children expired in excruciating tortures.

The next attempt was upon the life of her mistress, Mrs. Eccleston, who, after sustaining torments undescribable, with great difficulty recovered; but she continues in a state that leaves little hope that she will ever enjoy the blessing of health—such a shock has a delicate constitution suffered!

Four children were actually killed, and the life of a fifth person nearly sacrificed. Where this horrid business would have terminated, God only knows, if by his divine interposition the hellish purpose had not been arrested where it was.

Murder with an Ax*

The gallows were standing at Marksville [Louisiana] last January, upon which one [slave] was executed a year ago for killing his overseer. It occurred not many miles from Epps' plantation on Red River. The slave was given his task at splitting rails. In the course of the day the overseer sent him on an errand, which occupied so much time that it was not possible for him to perform the task. The next day he was called to an account, but the loss of time occasioned by the errand was no excuse, and he was ordered to kneel and bare his back for the reception of the lash. They were in the woods alone—beyond the reach of sight or hearing. The boy submitted until maddened at such injustice, and insane with pain, he sprang to his feet, and seizing an axe, literally chopped the overseer in pieces. He made no attempt whatever at concealment, but hastening to his master, related the whole affair, and declared himself ready to expiate the wrong by the sacrifice of his life. He was led to the scaffold, and while the rope was around his neck, maintained an undismayed and fearless bearing, and with his last words justified the act.

---

* Sue Eakin and Joseph Logsdon, eds., *Twelve Years a Slave*, by Solomon Northup (Baton Rouge, Louisiana, 1968), pp. 170–171.

Aunt Sallie Hung for Murder*

The people that owned the plantation near us had lots of slaves. They owned lots of my kinfolks. They master would beat 'em at night when they come from the field and lock 'em up. He'd whup 'em and send 'em to the field. They couldn't visit no slaves, and no slaves was 'lowed to visit 'em. So my cousin Sallie watched him hide the keys. So she moved 'em a little further back so that he had to lean over to reach 'em. That morning soon when he come to let 'em out, she cracked him in the head with the poker and made Little Joe help put his head in the fireplace. That day in the field Little Joe made a song: "If you don't believe Aunt Sallie kilt Marse Jim, the blood is on her underdress." He just hollered it, "Aunt Sallie kilt Marse Jim." They 'zamined Aunt Sallie's underdress, so they put her in jail till the baby come, then they tried her and sentenced her to hung, and she was.

---

* B. A. Botkin, ed., *Lay My Burden Down: A Folk History of Slavery* (Chicago, 1965), p. 174.

Chapter Five

Slave Insurrections, North and South

SECTION 1. TWO CONSPIRATORIAL LETTERS

Since the possibility of slave revolts caused intense fear and suspicion among whites during the entire period of slavery, conspirators
were required to use the utmost caution in communicating with each
other. Furthermore, to impede the process of organization and planning
necessary to a successful insurrection (as well as to protect the slaves
from contact with inflammatory information and ideas), the slaveholders
made it as difficult as possible for blacks to learn reading and writing.

Not surprisingly, then, few letters written by black revolutionaries
to their fellows have ever been found. The first of the two letters
printed below was picked up on the street in Yorktown, Virginia, in
August 1793. The second turned up on a road in Halifax County, North
Carolina, in March 1810. Presented just as they were written, these
documents offer a poignant initial insight into the situation of the insur-
rectionist slave.

Virginia, ca. 1793*

Dear Friend—The great secret that has been so long in being with our
own color has come nearly to a head that some in our Town has told of
it but in such a slight manner it is not believed, we have got about
five hundred Guns aplenty of lead but not much powder, I hope you

---

* Manuscript, South Carolina Historical Commission, Columbia, South
Carolina.

have made a good collection of powder and ball and will hold yourself
in readiness to strike whenever called for and never be out of the way
it will not be long before it will take place, and I am fully satisfied we
shall be in full possession of the whole country in a few weeks, since
I wrote you last I got a letter from our friend in Charleston he tells
me he has listed near six thousand men, there is a gentleman that says
he will give us as much powder as we want and when we begin he will
help us all he can, the damn'd brutes patroles is going all night in
Richmond but will soon cill [kill] them all, there an't many, we will
appoint a night to begin with fire clubs and shot, we will kill all before
us, it will begin in every town in one nite   Keep ready to receive
orders, when I hear from Charleston again I shall no and will rite to
you, he that give you this is a good friend and don't let any body see
it, rite me by the same hand he will give it to me out his hand he will
be up next week don't be feared have a good heart fight brave and
we will get free, I had like to get each [unreadable word] but God was
for me, and I got away, no more now but remain your friend—Secret
Keeper Richmond to secret keeper Norfolk.

Georgia, ca. 1810*

Dear Sir—I received your letter to the fourteenth of June, 1809 with
great freedom and joy to hear and understand what great proceedance
you have made, and the resolution you have in proceeding on in business as we have undertook, and hope you will still continue in the same
mind. We have spread the sense nearly over the continent in our part
of the country, and have the day when we are to fall to work, and you
must be sure not to fail on that day and that is the 22nd April, to begin
about midnight, and do the work at home first, and then take the
armes of them you slay first, and that will strengthen us more in armes
—for freedom we want and will have, for we have served this cruel
land long enuff, & be as secret convaing your nuse as possabel, and be
sure to send it by some cearfull hand, and if it happens to be discovered,
fail not in the day, for we are full abel to conquer by any means.—Sir,
I am your Captain James, living in the state of Jorgy, in Green county—
so no more at present, but remaining your sincer friend and captain
until death.

---

* Written by a slave in Greene County, Georgia to one Cornell Lucas in Martin
County, North Carolina. *New York Evening Post* (April 30, 1910).

SECTION 2. CONSPIRACY IN NEW YORK CITY, 1712

Shortly after the midnight of April 6, 1712, some two dozen slaves, having bound themselves "to secrecy by Sucking ye blood of each other's hand," confronted the white citizens of New York City with the first serious slave insurrection in colonial America. Here is Governor Robert Hunter's report to the British Lords of Trade on the "bloody conspiracy."

Governor Hunter's Report*

I must now give your Lordships an account of a bloody conspiracy of some of the slaves of this place, to destroy as many of the Inhabitants as they could. It was put in execution in this manner: when they had resolved to revenge themselves for some hard usage they apprehended to have received from their masters (for I can find no other cause), they agreed to meet in the orchard of Mr. Crook the middle of the Town—some provided with fire arms, some with swords and others with knives and hatchets. This was the sixth day of April; the time of meeting was about twelve or one o'clock in the night, when about three and twenty of them were got togeather. One Coffee and negroe slave to one Vantiburgh set fire to an out house of his Master's, and then repairing to the place where the rest were they all sallyed out togeather with their arms and marched to the fire. By this time, the noise of fire spreading through the town, the people began to flock to it; upon the approach of severall the slaves fired and killed them. The noise of the guns gave the allarm, and some, escaping their shot, soon published the cause of the fire, which was the reason that not above nine Christians [whites] were killed, and about five or six wounded. Upon the first notice, which was very soon after the mischeif was begun, I order'd a detachment from the fort under a proper officer to march against them, but the slaves made their retreat into the woods by the favour of the night. Having ordered centries the next day in the most proper places on the Island to prevt their escape, I caused, the day following, the Militia of this town and of the county of west Chester to drive the Island; and by this means and strick searches in the town,

---

* E. B. O'Callaghan, *Documents Relative to the Colonial History of the State of New York*, vol. 5 (Albany, 1855), pp. 341–342. Punctuation altered.

we found all that put the design in execution. Six of these having first laid violent hands upon themselves, the rest were forthwith brought to their tryal before ye Justices of this place who are authorized by Act of Assembly to hold a Court in such cases. In that Court were twenty seven condemned, whereof twenty one were executed; one being a woman with child, her execution [was] by that means suspended. Some were burnt, others hanged, one broke on the wheele, and one hung a live in chains in the town, so that there has been the most exemplary punishment inflicted that could be possibly thought of, and which only this act of assembly could Justify. Among these guilty persons several others were apprehended and again acquitted by the Court for want of sufficient evidence. Among those was one Mars, a negroe man slave to one Mr Regnier, who was [taken] to his tryall and acquitted by the Jury—the Sheriffe the next day moving the Court for the discharge of such as were or should be soe acquitted, by reason hee apprehended they would attempt to make their excape [from jail]; but Mr Bickley, who yn [then] executed the office of the Atter: Generall, [out of hostility] for Mr Rayner [Regnier] opposed his [the sheriff's] motion, telling the Court that at that time, none but Mars being acquitted, the motion could be only intended in his [Mars'] favour, against whom he [Bickley] should have some thing further to object [charge], and therefore prayed he might not be discharg[ed]; so the sheriff did not obtain his motion. Mars was then indicted a second time and again acquitted but not discharg'd; and, being a third time presented, was transferr'd (the Court of Justices not designing to sit again) to the supream Court and there tryed and convicted on ye same evidence [as given] on his two former tryals. This prosecution was carryed on to gratify some private pique of Mr Bickleys against Mr Regnier, a gentleman of his own profession, which [trial] appearing so partial, and the evidence being represented to me as very defective, and [Mars] being wholly acquitted of ever having known any thing of the Conspiracy by the Negroe witnesses who were made use of in the tryals of all the criminals before the Justices (and without whose testimonies very few could have been punished), I thought fit to reprieve him till Her Majesties pleasure be known therein. In this supream court were likewise tryed one Husea belonging to Mrs Wenham, and one John belonging Mr Vantilbourgh—and convicted; these two are prisoners taken in a Spanish prize this war and brought into this Port by a Privateer about six or seven years agoe; and by reason of their colour, which is swarthy, they were said to be slaves and as such were sold among many others of the same colour and country; these two I have likewise reprieved till Her Majesties pleasure be signified. Soon after my arrival in this government I received petitions from several of these Spanish Indians, as they are called here, representing to me that they were free men, subjects to the King of Spain but sold here as slaves; I secretely pittyed their condition but, haveing no other evidence of wt [what] they asserted then [than] their own words, I had it not in my power to releive them. I am informed that in the West Indies, where their laws against their slaves are most severe, that in case of a conspiracy in which many are engaged a few only are executed for an example. In this case 21 are executed, and six having done that Justice on themselves, more have suffered than we can find were active in this bloody affair—which are reasons for my repreiving these; and if your Lordships think them of sufficient weight, I beg you will procure Her Majesty's pleasure to be signifyed to me for their pardon, for they lye now in prison at their masters charge. I have likewise reprcived one Tom, a Ncgroc belonging to mr Van Dam, and Coffee a Negroe belonging to Mr Walton; these two I have repreived at the instance of the Justices of the Court, who where of oppinion that the evidence against them was not sufficient to convict them.

SECTION 3.   SOUTH CAROLINA, 1739

Rebellions occurred in the colonial South as well as in the North, particularly in Virginia and South Carolina. On September 9, 1739, at Stono, twenty miles southwest of Charleston, a band of slaves led by Jeremy (often referred to as Cato), killed an undisclosed number of whites, burned several buildings, and, "with Colours displayed and two Drums beating," set their route of march for Florida. Not far from Stono, they were met by the militia. Alexander Hcwatt, who arrived in the colonies in 1763, tells the outcome in the account below, taken from his 1779 history of Georgia and South Carolina.

Alexander Hewatt on the Stono Rebellion*

While Carolina was kept in a state of constant fear and agitation from this quarter, an insurrection openly broke out in the heart of the settlement, which alarmed the whole province. A number of

---

* From Alexander Hewatt, *An Historical Account of the Rise and Progress of the Colonies of South Carolina and Georgia*, vol. 2 (London, 1779), pp. 72–74; punctuation slightly changed.

negroes, having assembled together at Stono, first surprised and killed two young men in a warehouse and then plundered it of guns and ammunition. Being thus provided with arms, they elected one of their number captain, and agreed to follow him, marching towards the south-west with colours flying and drums beating, like a disciplined company. They forcibly entered the house of Mr. Godfrey, and having murdered him, his wife, and children, they took all the arms he had in it, set fire to the house, and then proceeded towards Jacksonsburgh. In their way they plundered and burnt every house, among which were those of Sacheveral, Nash, and Spry, killing every white person they found in them, and compelling the negroes to join them. Governor Bull, returning to Charlestown from the southward, met them and, observing them armed, quickly rode out of their way. He spread the alarm, which soon reached the Presbyterian church at Wiltown, where Archibald Stobo was preaching to a numerous congregation of planters in that quarter. By a law of the province all planters were obliged to carry their arms to church, which at this critical juncture proved a very useful and necessary regulation. The women were left in church trembling with fear while the militia, under the command of Captain Bee, marched in quest of the negroes, who by this time had become formidable from the number that joined them. They had marched above twelve miles and spread desolation through all the plantations in their way. Having found rum in some houses and drank freely of it, they halted in an open field and began to sing and dance by way of triumph. During these rejoicings the militia discovered them and stationed themselves in different places around them, to prevent them from making their escape. The intoxication of several of the slaves favoured the assailants. One party [of planters] advanced into the open field and attacked them, and, having killed some negroes, the remainder [of the Negroes] took to the woods and were dispersed. Many ran back to their plantations, in hopes of escaping suspicion from the absence of their masters; but the greater part were taken and tried. Such as had been compelled to join them contrary to their inclination were pardoned, but all the chosen leaders and first insurgents suffered death.

All Carolina was struck with terror and consternation by this insurrection, in which above twenty persons were murdered before it was quelled, and had not the people in that quarter been fortunately collected together at church it is probable many more would have suffered. Or had it become general, the whole colony must have fallen a sacrifice to their great power and indiscriminate fury. It was commonly believed, and not without reason, that the Spaniards [who then possessed Florida] were deeply concerned in promoting the mischief, and by their secret influence and intrigues with slaves had instigated them to this massacre. Having already four companies of negroes in their service, by penetrating into Carolina and putting the province into confusion they might no doubt have raised many more. But, to prevent further attempts, Governor Bull sent an express to General Oglethorpe with advice of the insurrection, desiring him to double his vigilance in Georgia, and seize all straggling Spaniards and negroes. In consequence of which a proclamation was issued to stop all slaves found in that province, offering a reward for every one they might catch attempting to run off. At the same time a company of rangers were employed to patrole the frontiers and block up all passages by which they might make their escape to Florida.

SECTION 4.   VIRGINIA, 1800

Governor James Monroe of Virginia, in a letter to his good friend Thomas Jefferson, called the Gabriel revolt "unquestionably the most serious and formidable conspiracy we have ever known of the kind." Tall, youthful "General" Gabriel belonged to a slaveholder reputed to have treated his slaves with "great barbarity." Gabriel assembled an indeterminate number of "bold adventurers," as Monroe put it, and prepared to take Richmond, evidently relying on a successful first strike to bring additional allies. A tremendous rain that kept the slaves from reaching Richmond, and betrayal by two of their number, terminated the dream. In an atmosphere of great secrecy, to prevent panic, the trials were held and executions carried out promptly. Governor Monroe reported the whole affair in a long letter to the speakers of the General Assembly.

James Monroe: General Gabriel's Revolt*

RICHMOND, DECEMBER 5th, 1800

SIRS,—An important incident has occurred since your last session, which I consider it my duty to submit fully and accurately in all its details to the wisdom of the General Assembly. On the 30th of August,

* From *The Writings of James Monroe*, ed., Stanislaus Murray Hamilton, vol. 3 (New York, 1900), pp. 234–243; punctuation slightly changed.

about two in the afternoon, Mr. Moseby Shephard, a respectable citizen of this county, called and informed me he had just received advice from two slaves that the negroes in the neighbourhood of Thomas H. Prosser intended to rise that night, kill their masters, and proceed to Richmond where they would be joined by the negroes of the city; that they would then take possession of the arms, ammunition, and the town. He added he had long known these two slaves and had no doubt of the truth of the information they gave him, and that he communicated it to me that the proposed insurrection might be defeated if possible. This communication was very interesting, and the source from whence derived calculated to inspire a belief it was true. The day was far advanced when I received it, so that if any provision was to be made to avert the danger not a moment was to be lost. I immediately called in the officers commanding the regiment of Militia & troop of Cavalry in town and made the best disposition for such an emergency the time would allow. A guard of a Captain and thirty men was placed at the Penitentiary where the publick arms were deposited, twenty at the Magazine, and fifteen at the Capitol, and the Horse was ordered to patrol the several routes leading to the city from Mr. Prosser's estate, and to apprize me without delay if anything like a movement of the negroes was seen, or other circumstance creating a suspicion such was contemplated. The close of the day was marked by one of the most extraordinary falls of rain ever known in our country. Every animal sought shelter from it. Nothing occurred in the night, of the kind suspected, to disturb the tranquility of the city, and in the morning the officer commanding the Horse reported he had seen but one circumstance unusual in the neighbourhood, which was that all the negroes he passed on the road in the intervals of the storm were going from the town, whereas it was their custom to visit it every Saturday night. This circumstance was not otherwise important th[e]n as it was said the first rendezvous of the negroes was to be in the country. The same precautions were observed the next night against the threatened insurrection and the same report made the next day by the officers on duty, so that I was on the point of concluding there was no foundation for the alarm when I was informed by Major Mosby and other gentlemen of character from his neighborhood [that] they were satisfied a project of insurrection, such as above described, did exist, and that the parties to it meant still to carry it into effect. These gentlemen stated facts and gave details which left no doubt in my mind of the existence of such a project. From this period the affair assumed a more important aspect. It did not seem probable the slaves in this city and neighbourhood would undertake so bold an enterprise without support from the slaves in other quarters of the State. It was more reasonable to presume an extensive combination had been formed among them for that purpose. Heretofore I had endeavoured to give the affair as little importance as the measures necessary for defence would permit. I had hoped it would even pass unnoticed by the community. But as soon as I was satisfied a conspiracy existed, it became my duty to estimate the crisis according to its magnitude and to take regular and systematic measures to avert the danger. In consequence I issued a summons to convene the Council at ten the next day, and in the interim advised the gentlemen who gave me the information to apprehend and commit to prison without delay all the slaves in the county whose guilt they had good cause to suspect. . . . In the evening of the same day about twenty of the conspirators were brought to town from Mr. Prosser's and the neighbouring estates, and as the jail could not contain them they were lodged in the Penitentiary. The chiefs were not to be found. Some of the arms which they had prepared for the occasion, formed of scythe blades, well calculated for execution, were likewise brought with them. By the information now received, as by former communications, it appeared that the inhabitants of that neighbourhood were in a particular degree exposed to danger; the conspiracy commenced with their slaves, and they were to be its first victims. . . . Every day now threw new light on this affair and increased the idea of its importance. . . . The trials had now commenced whereby the nature and extent of the conspiracy became better understood. It was satisfactorily proven that a general insurrection of the slaves was contemplated by those who took the lead in the affair. A species of organization had taken place among them. At a meeting held for the purpose, they had appointed a commander, to whom they gave the title of General, and had also appointed some other officers. They contemplated a force of cavalry as well as infantry, and had formed a plan of attack on the city which was to commence by setting fire to the lower end of the town where the houses consisted chiefly of wood, in expectation of drawing the people to that quarter while they assailed the Penitentiary, Magazine [arsenal] and Capitol, intending, after achieving these and getting possession of the arms, to meet the people unarmed on their return. The accounts of the number of those who were to commence the movement varied. Some made it considerable, others less so. It was distinctly seen that it embraced most of the slaves in this city and neighbourhood, and that the combination extended to several of the adjacent counties, Hanover, Caroline, Louisa, Chesterfield, and to the neighbourhood of the Point of Fork; and there was good cause to believe that the knowledge of such a project pervaded other parts, if not the whole State. At this time there was no reason to believe if such a project was ever conceived, that it was [now] abandoned. Those who gave the earliest information and were best informed on the subject thought otherwise. It was understood that the leaders in the conspiracy, who had absconded, were concealed in the neighbourhood. And as several of the parties to it were confined in the Jail condemned to suffer death, and many others in the Penitentiary [were] likely to experience the same fate, it was probable [that] sympathy for their associates might drive them [the remaining conspirators] to despair and prompt them to make a bolder effort for their relief. The opposite effect was expected from the measures pursued by the Government, but yet the result was uncertain. Other considerations presented themselves to view in weighing the part it was then incumbent on me to take. The number of slaves in this city and its neighbourhood, comprising those at work on the publick buildings, the canal, and the coal pits, was considerable. These might be assembled in a few hours, and could only be opposed by a respectable force, which force, if the city was surprised, could not be collected in a short time. The probability was if their first effort succeeded, we should see the town in flames, its inhabitants butchered, and a scene of horror extending through the country. This spectacle, it is true, would be momentary only, for as soon as a body of militia could be formed the insurrection would be suppressed. The superiority in point of numbers, in the knowledge and use of arms, and indeed every other species of knowledge which the whites have over the blacks in this Commonwealth, is so decisive that the latter could only sustain themselves for a moment in a rebellion against the former. Still it was a crisis to be avoided so far as prudent precautions could accomplish it. There was one other consideration which engaged the mind in the commencement of this affair from which it was not easy to withdraw it. It seemed strange that the slaves should embark in this novel and unexampled enterprise of their own accord. Their treatment has been more favorable since the revolution, and as the importation was prohibited among the first acts of our independence, their number has not increased in proportion with that of the whites. It was natural to suspect they were prompted to it by others who were invisible but whose agency might be powerful. And if this was the case it became proportionally more difficult to estimate the extent of the combination, and the consequent real importance of the crisis. On consideration of all these circumstances it was deemed necessary to call out such a force as might be fully adequate to the emergency—such an one as would likely to overawe and keep down the spirit of insurrection, or [would be] sufficient to supress it in case it broke out. On that principle I called into service on the 9th the 19th and 24d regiments, and a detachment of fifty men additional from the 33d; which detachment with the whole of the 19th regiment and one hundred men of the 23d, were ordered to take post in this city. The residue of the 23d were stationed in the town of Manchester. . . . It was paraded daily on the Capitol square, and trained as well that it might be prepared for action if occasion required as that our strength might be known to the conspirators. The effect which this measure produced was easily and soon perceived. It was evident that the collection and display of this force inspired the citizens with confidence, and depressed the spirits of the slaves. The former saw in it a security from the danger which menaced them; the latter a defeat of their nefarious projects. On the 12th of September, five, and on the fifteenth following, five others were executed. On those occasions the whole force in service in the city (infantry and horse) attended the execution. On the 27th Gabriel, one of the chiefs of the conspiracy, for whom a reward had been offered and who had been apprehended at Norfolk, was delivered up and committed to Jail. As these executions were carried into effect without any movement of the slaves, and their chief [was] apprehended, it was fair to presume the danger of the crisis had passed. It became from that period the object of the Executive to diminish the force with a view to lessen the expense, which object was pursued with undeviating attention. . . . It belongs to the Legislature to weigh with profound attention this unpleasant incident in our history. What has happened may occur again at any time with more fatal consequences, unless suitable measures be taken to prevent it. Unhappily while this class of people exists among us we can never count with certainty on its tranquil submission. The fortunate issue of the late attempt should not lull us into repose. It ought rather to stimulate us to the adoption of a system which, if it does not prevent the like in future, may secure the country from any calamitous consequences.

SECTION 5. THE VESEY CONSPIRACY, 1822

The Denmark Vesey plot in South Carolina in 1822, called the "most elaborate insurrectionary project ever formed by American slaves" by white abolitionist Thomas Wentworth Higginson, has been said to have involved as many as nine thousand men. State and local conditions undoubtedly stimulated the revolt, for, as Negro author William Wells Brown pointed out, South Carolina's measures to keep the black men down were quite the most oppressive of all the Southern states; accordingly, six uprisings in South Carolina between 1800 and 1821 have been turned up by Herbert Aptheker. Charleston, during the period of Vesey's organizing and recruiting, was beset by economic ailments; moreover, its white population was on the decline while its Negro residents were increasing to become well over half the city. Suspicious of the large assemblies of blacks in the local African Methodist churches, white authorities cracked down on a Sunday in 1818 by arresting one hundred forty persons at one of the churches (the church to which Denmark Vesey belonged) and placing them into the guardhouse, afterwards punishing the leaders with fines, imprisonment, or lashings.

Despite rigorous precautions, it was too much to expect that the boldly conceived plans of Vesey and his principal lieutenants, working together for well over a year, could remain secret. On May 25, 1822, on the Charleston waterfront, two slaves, William and Peter, struck up a casual conversation, during the course of which William told his new acquaintance that the slaves had decided to end their bondage by collective means. Peter told a free Negro and, on the freedman's advice, his own master. In the next weeks, rumors spread through Charleston as a special tribunal called witnesses and meted out punishment. Ultimately forty-two men were banished and thirty-five executed. Death was the lot of Denmark Vesey.

The documents that follow view the conspiracy from three perspectives. First there is the official testimony of Peter, the informer; next comes the testimony of Rolla, slave of the Governor of South Carolina and one of Vesey's closest associates; the final selection is an article written by Governor Thomas Bennett in the hope of calming the citizenry, who, he felt, had distorted the conspiracy out of all reasonable proportions. It should be noted here that one scholar, Richard Wade, in his *Slavery in the Cities* and "The Vesey Plot: A Reconsideration" (*Journal of Southern History* 12 [May, 1964], 143–161), argues that the plot "was probably never more than loose talk by aggrieved and embittered men."

Peter, the Informer*

On Saturday afternoon last (my master being out of town) I went to market; after finishing my business I strolled down the wharf below the fish market, from which I observed a small vessel in the stream with a singular flag; whilst looking at this object, a black man (Mr. Paul's William) came up to me and remarking the subject which engaged my attention said, "I have often seen a flag with the number 76 on it, but never with 96 before." After some trifling conversation on this point, he remarked with considerable earnestness to me. "Do you know that something serious is about to take place?" To which I replied, "No." "Well," said he, "there is, and many of us are determined to right ourselves!" I asked him to explain himself—when he remarked, "Why, we are determined to shake off our bondage, and for this purpose we stand on a good foundation; many have joined, and if you will go with me, I will show you the man who has the list of names who will take yours down." I was so much astonished and horror struck at this information, that it was a moment or two before I could collect myself sufficient to tell him I would have nothing to do with this business, that I was satisfied with my condition, that I was grateful to my master for his kindness and wished no change. I left him instantly, lest, if this fellow afterwards got into trouble and I had been seen conversing with him in so public a place, I might be suspected and thrown into difficulty. I did not, however, remain easy under the burden of such a secret, and consequently determined to consult a free man of colour named ——— and to ask his advice. On conferring with this friend, he urged me with great earnestness to communicate what had passed between Mr. Paul's man and myself to my master, and not lose a moment in so doing. I took his advice and, not waiting even for the return of my master to town, I mentioned it to my mistress and young master. On the arrival of my master, he examined me as to what had passed, and I stated to him what I have mentioned to yourselves.

Rolla's Statement

I know Denmark Vesey. On one occasion he asked me, "What news"; I told him, "None." He replied, "We are free but the white

---

* This testimony and the next are taken from *An Official Report of the Trials of Sundry Negroes, Charged with an Attempt to Raise an Insurrection in the State of South-Carolina* ..., prepared and published at the request of the Court, by Lionel H. Kennedy and Thomas Parker, members of the Charleston bar and the Presiding Magistrates of the Court (Charleston, 1822), pp. 48–51, 66–67. Punctuation has been altered slightly.

people here won't let us be so, and the only way is to rise up and fight the whites." I went to his house one night to learn where the meetings were held. I never conversed on this subject with Batteau or Ned— Vesey told me he was the leader in this plot. I never conversed either with Peter or Mingo. Vesey induced me to join; when I went to Vesey's house there was a meeting there, the room was full of people, but none of them white. That night at Vesey's we determined to have arms made, and each man put in twelve and one-half cents toward that purpose. Though Vesey's room was full I did not know one individual there. At this meeting Vesey said we were to take the Guard-House and Magazine to get arms; that we ought to rise up and speak, and he *read to us from the Bible, how the Children of Israel were delivered out of Egypt from bondage.* He said that the rising would take place, last Sunday night week (the 16th June), and that Peter Poras was one.

The Account of Governor Bennett*

On the 18th June ten slaves were arrested, and on the 19th the court was organized for their trial. Investigation was retarded by the difficulty of procuring authentic evidence, and it was not until the 28th that the sentence of death was pronounced against six of the persons charged with offence. Denmark Vesey, a free negro, was arrested on the 21st, and on the 22d put on his trial. Although he was unquestionably the instigator and chief of this plot, no positive proof of his guilt appeared until the 25th. This grew out of the confession of one of the convicts, and on the 27th his guilt was further established by a servant of Mr. Ferguson. . . .

. . . Having established the existence of a plot and the places of rendezvous, all that was deemed requisite for conviction was to prove an association with the ringleaders and an expression of their assent to the measure. On such [grounds], generally, the sentence of death has been executed. Others who, without actually combining, were proved to have known of the conspiracy and to have given their sanction by any act, have been sentenced to die and their punishment commuted to banishment from the United States; or [they have been] sentenced in the first instance to banishment from this state or from the United States. In this manner the whole number, seventy-two, have been disposed of: thirty-five executed and thirty-seven sentenced

* From *Niles' Register* (September 7, 1822), with minor punctuation change.

to banishment. With these we may reasonably conclude that we have reached the extremities of this conspiracy, and this opinion, if not conclusive, is entitled to great weight when we advert to the extraordinary measures pursued to effect the object, and the motives which influenced the accused. . . .

. . . Among the conspirators, the most daring and active was Monday, the slave of Mr. Gell. He could read and write with facility, and thus attained an extraordinary and dangerous influence over his fellows. Permitted by his owner to occupy a house in a central part of the city, hourly opportunities were afforded for the exercise of his skill on those who were attracted to his shop by business or favor. It was there that his artful and insidious delusions were kept in perpetual exercise. Materials were abundently furnished in the seditious pamphlets brought into this state by equally culpable incendiaries, while the speeches of the oppositionists in Congress to the admission of Missouri gave a serious and imposing effect to his machinations. This man wrote to Boyer (by his own confession) requesting his aid, and addressed the envelope of his letter to a relative of the person who became the bearer of it, a negro from one of the northern states. He was the only person proved to have kept a list of those engaged; and the court considered his confession full and ample. From such means and such sources of information, it cannot be doubted that all who were actually concerned have been brought to justice. There is no exception within my knowledge; it has, however, been stated that a plantation in St. John's was infected, but I do not know of what authority.

The plain detail of the principal incidents in this transaction will satisfy you that the scheme has not been general nor alarmingly extensive. And it furnishes a cause for much satisfaction that, although religion, superstition, fear, and almost every passion that sways the human mind have been artfully used by the wicked instigators of this design, so few have been seduced from a course of propriety and obedience. Those who associated were unprovided with the means of attack or resistance. No weapons (if we except thirteen hoop-poles) have been discovered, nor any testimony received but of six pikes, that such preparations were actually made. The witnesses generally agree in one fact, that the attempt was to have taken place on Sunday night the 16th of June, differing a little as to the precise time; 12 o'clock appears to have been the hour.

From the various conflicting statements made during the trials, it is difficult to form a plausible conjecture of their ultimate plans of operation; no two agreeing on general definite principles. That the first essay would be made with clubs against the state arsenal is infer-rable from their being unprovided with arms and the concurrence of several witnesses. But whether the attack would be made simultane-ously by various detachments, or whether the whole, embodied at a particular spot, would proceed to the accomplishment of their object, is very uncertain. Upon the whole, it is manifest that if any plan had been organized it was never communicated by the principal conspirator to the leaders or the men, as they were wholly ignorant even of the places of rendezvous; although [the plot was discovered] within two days of the time appointed and but one man [was] arrested prior to the day fixed on for the attempt.

SECTION 6.   NAT TURNER'S REBELLION

In the midst of the Civil War, William Wells Brown wrote, "Every eye is now turned towards the south, looking for another Nat Turner." A century later another Nat Turner did appear, the creation of novelist William Styron (The Confessions of Nat Turner, 1967), becoming an instant critical and commercial success and, at the same time, setting off a chorus of protests by black critics. Subsequently, Styron, a white Southerner, has been charged with being paternalistic and impercep-tive, a racist, a liar, and a poor researcher. Others have alleged that, as a modern-day existentialist, Styron does not understand the power of religion to the nineteenth-century Negro — furthermore, that he does not comprehend the revolutionary mind. The novel, they say, represents not the confessions of Nat Turner, but the confessions of William Styron.

At least some of Styron's difficulties stem from his having accepted, indeed, exaggerated, as did practically every white scholar and many black ones, the glamorous scholarship of the early 1960's. Specifically, he built into his work Stanley Elkins' idea of the infantilized slave and Daniel Moynihan's thesis of the weakness of the Negro family structure with its matriarchal center and its emasculated males. These views, now seriously questioned by scholars, are not geared to enhance the pride, dignity, and self-respect so valued by the black power movement, and Styron's popular attempt to graft them onto an authentic black hero evoked natural resentment in blacks.

Styron's novel, thus alternately blessed and damned, points up one of the crucial questions of this age: how much longer can we continue to view the Negro from the plantation house, several generations removed, without considering also the modern equivalent of the slave-quarters perspective.

The best source on Nat Turner, even filtered through the person of an understandably less-than-sympathetic white Southerner, is still Nat Turner himself. His confessions, as told by Thomas Gray, a court-appointed lawyer, are printed below in full.

Turner's Own Confession*

[*T.R.G.:*] Agreeable to his own appointment, on the evening he was committed to prison, with permission of the jailer, I visited Nat on Tuesday the 1st November, when, without being questioned at all, he commenced his narrative in the following words:

SIR,—You have asked me to give a history of the motives which induced me to undertake the late insurrection, as you call it. To do so I must go back to the days of my infancy, and even before I was born. I was thirty-one years of age the 2nd of October last, and born the property of Benj. Turner, of this county. In my childhood a circumstance occurred which made an indelible impression on my mind, and laid the ground work of that enthusiasm, which has terminated so fatally to many, both white and black, and for which I am about to atone at the gallows. It is here necessary to relate this circumstance—trifling as it may seem, it was the commencement of that belief which has grown with time, and even now, sir, in this dungeon, helpless and forsaken as I am, I cannot divest myself of. Being at play with other children when three or four years old, I was telling them something which my mother, overhearing, said it had happened before I was born; I stuck to my story, however, and related some things which went, in her opinion, to confirm it. Others being called on were greatly astonished, knowing that these things had happened, and [this] caused

---

* *The Confessions of Nat Turner, The Leader of the Late Insurrection in Southampton, Va.* As fully and voluntarily made to Thomas R. Gray, in the prison where he was confined, and acknowledged by him to be such when read before the court of Southampton; with the certificate, under seal of the Court convened at Jerusalem, Nov. 5, 1831, for his trial. Also, An Authentic Account of the Whole Insurrection, with lists of the whites who were murdered, and of the negroes brought before the court of Southampton, and there sentenced, &c. (Baltimore, 1831). Some changes in typography.

them to say in my hearing [that] I surely would be a prophet, as the Lord had shewn me things that had happened before my birth. And my father and mother strengthened me in this my first impression, saying in my presence [that] I was intended for some great purpose, which they had always thought from certain marks on my head and breast [A parcel of excrescences which I believe are not at all uncommon, particularly among negroes, as I have seen several with the same. In this case he has either cut them off or they have nearly disappeared. —T. R. G.]. My grandmother, who was very religious and to whom I was much attached; my master, who belonged to the church; and other religious persons who visited the house, and whom I often saw at prayers—[these people,] noticing the singularity of my manners, I suppose, and my uncommon intelligence for a child, remarked I had too much sense to be raised, and if I was, I would never be of any service to any one as a slave. To a mind like mine—restless, inquisitive, and observant of every thing that was passing—it is easy to suppose that religion was the subject to which it would be directed; and although this subject principally occupied my thoughts, there was nothing that I saw or heard of to which my attention was not directed. The manner in which I learned to read and write not only had great influence on my own mind, as I acquired it with the most perfect ease (so much so that I have no recollection whatever of learning the alphabet—but to the astonishment of the family, one day when a book was shewn to me to keep me from crying, I began spelling the names of different objects), this was a source of wonder [also] to all in the neighborhood, particularly the blacks; and this learning was constantly improved at all opportunities. When I got large enough to go to work, while employed I was reflecting on many things that would present themselves to my imagination, and whenever an opportunity occurred of looking at a book when the school children were getting their lessons, I would find many things that the fertility of my own imagination had depicted to me before. All my time not devoted to my master's service was spent either in prayer or in making experiments in casting different things in moulds made of earth, in attempting to make paper, gun-powder, and many other experiments that although I could not perfect, yet convinced me of its practicability if I had the means. [*Footnote in original source:* When questioned as to the manner of manufacturing those different articles, he was found well informed on the subject.] I was not addicted to stealing in my youth, nor have ever been. Yet such was the confidence of the negroes in the neighborhood, even at this early period of my life, in my superior judgment, that they would often carry me with them when they were going on any roguery, to plan for them. Growing up among them, with this confidence in my superior judgment, and when this, in their opinions, was perfected by Divine inspiration from the circumstances already alluded to in my infancy (and which belief was ever afterwards zealously inculcated by the austerity of my life and manners, which became the subject of remark by white and black)— having soon discovered [myself] to be great, I [realized] must [also] appear so, and therefore studiously avoided mixing in society and wrapped myself in mystery, devoting my time to fasting and prayer. By this time, having arrived to man's estate, and hearing the scriptures commented on at meetings, I was struck with that particular passage which says: "Seek ye the kingdom of Heaven and all things shall be added unto you." I reflected much on this passage, and prayed daily for light on this subject. As I was praying one day at my plough, the spirit spoke to me, saying "Seek ye the kingdom of Heaven and all things shall be added unto you."—*Question* [T. R. G.]: "What do you mean by the Spirit?" *Answer:* The Spirit that spoke to the prophets in former days.—And I was greatly astonished, and for two years prayed continually, whenever my duty would permit. And then again I had the same revelation, which fully confirmed me in the impression that I was ordained for some great purpose in the hands of the Almighty. Several years rolled round, in which many events occurred to strengthen me in this my belief. At this time I reverted in my mind to the remarks made of me in my childhood, and the things that had been shewn me; and as it had been said of me in my childhood by those by whom I had been taught to pray, both white and black, and in whom I had the greatest confidence, that I had too much sense to be raised, and if I was, I would never be of any use to any one as a slave—now finding I had arrived to man's estate and was a slave, and these revelations being made known to me, I began to direct my attention to this great object, to fulfil the purpose for which, by this time, I felt assured I was intended. Knowing the influence I had obtained over the minds of my fellow servants (not by the means of conjuring and such like tricks—for to them I always spoke of such things with contempt— but by the communion of the Spirit whose revelations I often communicated to them, and they believed and said my wisdom came from God), I now began to prepare them for my purpose, by telling them something was about to happen that would terminate in fulfilling the great promise that had been made to me. About this time I was placed under an overseer, from whom I ran away; and after remaining in the woods thirty days I returned, to the astonishment of the negroes on the plantation, who thought I had made my escape to some other part of the country, as my father had done before. But the reason of

my return was that the Spirit appeared to me and said I had my wishes
directed to the things of this world and not to the kingdom of Heaven,
and that I should return to the service of my earthly master—"For
he who knoweth his Master's will, and doeth it not, shall be beaten with
many stripes, and thus have I chastened you." And the negroes found
fault, and murmured against me, saying that if they had my sense they
would not serve any master in the world. And about this time I had a
vision—and I saw white spirits and black spirits engaged in battle,
and the sun was darkened—the thunder rolled in the Heavens, and
blood flowed in streams—and I heard a voice saying, "Such is your luck,
such you are called to see, and let it come rough or smooth, you must
surely bare it." I now withdrew myself as much as my situation would
permit, from the intercourse of my fellow servants, for the avowed
purpose of serving the Spirit more fully; and it appeared to me, and
reminded me of the things it had already shown me, and [said] that it
would then reveal to me the knowledge of the elements, the revolution
of the planets, the operation of tides, and changes of the seasons. After
this revelation in the year of 1825, and the knowledge of the elements
being made known to me, I sought more than ever to obtain true
holiness before the great day of judgment should appear, and then I
began to receive the true knowledge of faith. And from the first steps
of righteousness until the last was I made perfect; and the Holy Ghost
was with me, and said, "Behold me as I stand in the Heavens"—and
I looked and saw the forms of men in different attitudes—and there
were lights in the sky to which the children of darkness gave other
names than what they really were, for they were the lights of the
Savior's hands, stretched forth from east to west, even as they were
extended on the cross on Calvary for the redemption of sinners. And
I wondered greatly at these miracles, and prayed to be informed of a
certainty of the meaning thereof. And shortly afterwards, while laboring in the field, I discovered drops of blood on the corn as though it
were dew from heaven, and I communicated it to many, both white
and black, in the neighborhood. And I then found on the leaves in the
woods hieroglyphic characters and numbers, with the forms of men in
different attitudes portrayed in blood and representing the figures I
had seen before in the heavens. And now the Holy Ghost had revealed
itself to me and made plain the miracles it had shown me. For as the
blood of Christ had been shed on this earth and had ascended to heaven
for the salvation of sinners, and was now returning to earth again in
the form of dew—and as the leaves on the trees bore the impression of
the figures I had seen in the heavens—it was plain to me that the Savior

was about to lay down the yoke he had borne for the sins of men, and the great day of judgment was at hand. About this time I told these things to a white man [Etheldred T. Brantley—T. R. G.] on whom it had a wonderful effect, and he ceased from his wickedness and was attacked immediately with a cutaneous eruption, and blood oozed from the pores of his skin; and after praying and fasting nine days, he was healed. And the Spirit appeared to me again and said [that] as the Savior had been baptised so should we be also; and when the white people would not let us be baptised by the church, we went down into the water together, in the sight of many who reviled us, and were baptised by the Spirit. After this I rejoiced greatly, and gave thanks to God. And on the 12th of May, 1828, I heard a loud noise in the heavens, and the Spirit instantly appeared to me and said the Serpent was loosened and Christ had laid down the yoke he had borne for the sins of men, and that I should take it on and fight against the Serpent, for the time was fast approaching when the first should be last and the last should be first.—*Question:* "Do you not find yourself mistaken now?" *Answer:* Was not Christ crucified? —And by signs in the Heavens [the Spirit said] that it would make known to me when I should commence the great work, and until the first sign appeared I should conceal it from the knowledge of men; and on the appearance of the sign (the eclipse of the sun last February) I should arise and prepare myself, and slay my enemies with their own weapons. And immediately on the sign appearing in the heavens the seal was removed from my lips, and I communicated the great work laid out for me to do, to four in whom I had the greatest confidence (Henry, Hark, Nelson, and Sam). It was intended by us to have begun the work of death on the 4th July last. Many were the plans formed and rejected by us, and it affected my mind to such a degree that I fell sick and the time passed without our coming to any determination how to commence. [We were] still forming new schemes and rejecting them when the sign appeared again, which determined me not to wait longer.

Since the commencement of 1830, I had been living with Mr. Joseph Travis, who was to me a kind master, and placed the greatest confidence in me; in fact, I had no cause to complain of his treatment to me. On Saturday evening the 20th of August it was agreed between Henry, Hark, and myself to prepare a dinner the next day for the men we expected and then to concert a plan, as we had not yet determined on any. Hark on the following morning brought a pig, and Henry brandy, and being joined by Sam, Nelson, Will, and Jack, they prepared in the woods a dinner, where, about three o'clock, I joined them.

Q. "Why were you so backward in joining them?"

A. The same reason that had caused me not to mix with them for years before.

I saluted them on coming up, and asked Will how came he there; he answered, his life was worth no more than others, and his liberty as dear to him. I asked him if he thought to obtain it? He said he would, or lose his life. This was enough to put him in full confidence. Jack, I knew, was only a tool in the hands of Hark. It was quickly agreed we should commence at home [Mr. J. Travis'—T. R. G.] on that night, and until we had armed and equipped ourselves and gathered sufficient force, neither age nor sex was to be spared (which was invariably adhered to). We remained at the feast, until about two hours in the night, when we went to the house and found Austin; they all went to the cider press and drank, except myself. On returning to the house, Hark went to the door with an axe for the purpose of breaking it open, as we knew we were strong enough to murder the family if they were awaked by the noise; but, reflecting that it might create an alarm in the neighborhood, we determined to enter the house secretly and murder them whilst sleeping. Hark got a ladder and set it against the chimney, on which I ascended and, hoisting a window, entered and came down stairs, unbarred the door, and removed the guns from their places. It was then observed that I must spill the first blood. On which, armed with a hatchet and accompanied by Will, I entered my master's chamber; it being dark, I could not give a death blow: the hatchet glanced from his head. He sprang from the bed and called his wife; it was his last word. Will laid him dead with a blow of his axe, and Mrs. Travis shared the same fate as she lay in bed. The murder of this family, five in number, was the work of a moment; not one of them awoke. There was a little infant sleeping in a cradle that was forgotten until we had left the house and gone some distance, when Henry and Will returned and killed it. We got here four guns that would shoot and several old muskets, with a pound or two of powder. We remained some time at the barn, where we paraded; I formed them in a line as soldiers and, after carrying them through all the manoeuvres I was master of, marched them off to Mr. Salathul Francis', about six hundred yards distant. Sam and Will went to the door and knocked. Mr. Francis asked who was there; Sam replied it was him, and he had a letter for him, on which he got up and came to the door. They immediately seized him and, dragging him out a little from the door, he was dispatched by repeated blows on the head; there was no other white person in the family. We started from there for Mrs. Reese's (maintaining the most perfect silence on our march),

where, finding the door unlocked, we entered and murdered Mrs. Reese
in her bed while [she was] sleeping; her son awoke, but it was only to
sleep the sleep of death; he had only time to say "Who is that?" and
he was no more. From Mrs. Reese's we went to Mrs. Turner's, a mile
distant, which we reached about sunrise on Monday morning. Henry,
Austin, and Sam went to the still, where, finding Mr. Peebles, Austin
shot him, and the rest of us went to the house; as we approached, the
family discovered us and shut the door. Vain hope! Will, with one
stroke of his axe, opened it, and we entered and found Mrs. Turner and
Mrs. Newsome in the middle of a room almost frightened to death.
Will immediately killed Mrs. Turner with one blow of his axe. I took
Mrs. Newsome by the hand, and with the sword I had when I was
apprehended I struck her several blows over the head—but not being
able to kill her, as the sword was dull. Will turning around and, discovering it, despatched her also. A general destruction of property
and search for money and ammunition always succeded the murders.
By this time my company amounted to fifteen, and nine men mounted,
who started for Mrs. Whitehead's (the other six were to go through a
by way to Mr. Bryant's and rejoin us at Mrs. Whitehead's). As we
approached the house we discovered Mr. Richard Whitehead standing
in the cotton patch near the lane fence; we called him over into the
lane, and Will, the executioner, was near at hand with his fatal axe
to send him to an untimely grave. As we pushed on to the house I
discovered some one run round the garden and, thinking it was some
of the white family, I pursued them; but finding it was a servant girl
belonging to the house I returned to commence the work of death.
But they whom I left had not been idle; all the family were already
murdered but Mrs. Whitehead and her daughter Margaret. As I came
round to the door I saw Will pulling Mrs. Whitehead out of the house,
and at the step he nearly severed her head from her body with his
broad axe. Miss Margaret, when I discovered her, had concealed herself in the corner formed by the projection of cellar cap from the house;
on my approach she fled but was soon overtaken, and after repeated
blows with a sword I killed her by a blow on the head with a fence
rail. By this time the six who had gone to Mr. Bryant's rejoined us
and informed me they had done the work of death assigned them. We
again divided, part going to Mr. Richard Porter's and from thence to
Nathaniel Francis', the others to Mr. Howell Harris' and Mr. T.
Doyle's. On my reaching Mr. Porter's, he had escaped with his family.
I understood there that the alarm had already spread, and I immediately returned to bring up those sent to Mr. Doyle's and Mr. Howell
Harris'; the party [I had started with,] I left going on to Mr. Francis',

having told them I would join them in that neighborhood. I met these sent to Mr. Doyles' and Mr. Harris' returning, having met Mr. Doyle on the road and killed him; and learning from some who joined them that Mr. Harris was [away] from home, I immediately pursued the course taken by the party gone on before; but knowing they would complete the work of death and pillage at Mr. Francis' before I could get there, I went to Mr. Peter Edwards' expecting to find them there, but they had been here also. I then went to Mr. John T. Barrow's; they had been here and murdered him. I pursued on their track to Captain Newit Harris', where I found the greater part mounted and ready to start [off again]; the men, now amounting to about forty, shouted and hurraed as I rode up; some were in the yard loading their guns, others drinking. They said Captain Harris and his family had escaped; the property in the house they destroyed, robbing him of money and other valuables. I ordered them to mount and march instantly. This was about nine or ten o'clock Monday morning. I proceeded to Mr. Levi Waller's, two or three miles distant. I took my station in the rear and, as it was my object to carry terror and devastation wherever we went, I placed fifteen or twenty of the best armed and most relied-on in front, who generally approached the houses as fast as their horses could run; this was [done for] two purposes: to prevent escape, and strike terror to the inhabitants. On this account I never got to the houses, after leaving Mrs. Whitehead's, until the murders were committed, except in one case. I sometimes got in sight in time to see the work of death completed, viewed the mangled bodies as they lay in silent satisfaction, and immediately started in quest of other victims. Having murdered Mrs. Waller and ten children, we started for Mr. William Williams'. Having killed him and two little boys that were there [dangling clause]; while [we were] engaged in this, Mrs. Williams fled and got some distance from the house; but she was pursued, overtaken, and compelled to get up behind one of the company, who brought her back; and after showing her the mangled body of her lifeless husband, she was told to get down and lay by his side, where she was shot dead. I then started for Mr. Jacob Williams, where the family were murdered. Here [we] found a young man named Drury, who had come on business with Mr. Williams—he was pursued, overtaken and shot. Mrs. Vaughan was the next place we visited, and after murdering the family here, I determined on starting for Jerusalem. Our number amounted now to fifty or sixty, all mounted and armed with guns, axes, swords and clubs. On reaching Mr. James W. Parker's gate immediately on the road leading to Jerusalem and about three miles distant, it was proposed to me to call there, but I objected as I knew he was gone to Jerusalem and my object was to reach there as soon as possible; but some of the men having relations at Mr. Parker's it was agreed that they might call and get his people. I remained at the gate on the road with seven or eight, the others going across the field to the house about half a mile off. After waiting some time for them I became impatient and started to the house for them; and on our return we were met by a party of white men, who had pursued our blood-stained track and who had fired on those at the gate and dispersed them, which I knew nothing of, not having been at that time rejoined by any of them. Immediately on discovering the whites, I ordered my men to halt and form, as they appeared to be alarmed. The white men, eighteen in number, approached us in about one hundred yards, when one of them fired [This was against the positive orders of Captain Alexander P. Peete who commanded, and who had directed the men to reserve their fire until within thirty paces—T. R. G] and I discovered about half of them retreating. I then ordered my men to fire and rush on them; the few remaining stood their ground until we approached within fifty yards, when they fired and retreated. We pursued and overtook some of them who we thought we left dead [they were not killed —T. R. G.]; after pursuing them about two hundred yards and rising a little hill, I discovered they were met by another party and had halted and were reloading their guns. [This was a small party from Jerusalem who knew the negroes were in the field, and had just tied their horses to await their return to the road, knowing that Mr. Parker and family were in Jerusalem; but knew nothing of the party that had gone in with Captain Peete; on hearing the firing they immediately rushed to the spot and arrived just in time to arrest the progress of these barbarous villains and save the lives of their friends and fellow citizens—T. R. G.]. [I was] thinking that those who [had] retreated first and the party who [had] fired on us at fifty or sixty yards distant had all fallen back to meet others with ammunition. As I saw them reloading their guns—and more coming up than I saw at first, and several of my bravest men being wounded—the others became panick struck and squandered over the field; the white men pursued and fired on us several times. Hark had his horse shot under him, and I caught another for him as it was running by me; five or six of my men were wounded but none [were] left on the field. Finding myself defeated here I instantly determined to go through a private way and cross the Nottoway river at the Cypress Bridge, three miles below Jerusalem, and attack that place in the rear, as I expected they would look for me on the other road, and I had a great desire to get there [Jerusalem] to procure arms and ammunition. After going a short distance in this private way accompanied by about twenty men, I overtook two or three who told me the others were dispersed in every direction. After trying in vain to collect a sufficient force to proceed to Jerusalem I determined to return, as I was sure they would make back to their old neighborhood, where they would rejoin me, make new recruits, and come down again. On my way back, I called at Mrs. Thomas's, Mrs. Spencer's, and several other places; the white families having fled, we found no more victims to gratify our thirst for blood. We stopped at Maj. Ridley's quarter [neighborhood] for the night, and being joined by four of his men, with the recruits made since my defeat, we mustered now about forty strong. After placing out sentinels, I laid down to sleep but was quickly roused by a great racket; starting up, I found some mounted and others in great confusion, one of the sentinels having given the alarm that we were about to be attacked. I ordered some to ride round and reconnoitre, and on their return the others, being more alarmed (not knowing who they were), fled in different ways, so that I was reduced to about twenty again; with this I determined to attempt to recruit, and proceed on to rally in the neighborhood I had left. Dr. Blunt's was the nearest house, which we reached just before day; on riding up the yard, Hark fired a gun. We expected Dr. Blunt and his family were at Maj. Ridley's, as I knew there was a company of men there; the gun was fired to ascertain if any of the family were at home. We were immediately fired upon and retreated, leaving several of my men. I do not know what became of them as I never saw them afterwards. Pursuing our course back and coming in sight of Captain Harris', where we had been the day before, we discovered a party of white men at the house, on which all deserted me but two [Jacob and Nat—T. R. G.]. We concealed ourselves in the woods until near night, when I sent them in search of Henry, Sam, Nelson, and Hark, and directed them to rally all they could at the place we had had our dinner the Sunday before, where they would find me. And I accordingly returned there as soon as it was dark and remained until Wednesday evening, when, discovering white men riding around the place as though they were looking for some one, and none of my men joining me, I concluded Jacob and Nat had been taken and compelled to betray me. On this I gave up all hope for the present; and on Thursday night, after having supplied myself with provisions from Mr. Travis's, I scratched a hole under a pile of fence rails in a field, where I concealed myself for six weeks, never leaving my hiding place but for a few minutes in the dead of night to get water which was very near. Thinking by this time I could venture out, I began to go about in the night and eaves-drop the houses in the neighborhood, pursuing this course for about a fortnight and gathering little or no intelligence, afraid of speaking to any human being, and returning every morning to my cave before the dawn of day. I know not how long I might have led this life if accident had not betrayed me. A dog in the neighborhood, passing by my hiding place one night while I was out, was attracted by some meat I had in my cave and crawled in and stole it, and was coming out just as I returned. A few nights after, two negroes having started to go hunting with the same dog and [having] passed that way, the dog came again to the place; and [me] having just gone out to walk about, [he] discovered me and barked, on which, thinking myself discovered, I spoke to them to beg concealment. On making myself known they fled from me. Knowing then they would betray me, I immediately left my hiding place and was pursued almost incessantly until I was taken a fortnight afterwards by Mr. Benjamin Phipps, in a little hole I had dug out with my sword for the purpose of concealment under the top of a fallen tree. On Mr. Phipps' discovering the place of my concealment, he cocked his gun and aimed at me. I requested him not to shoot and [said that] I would give up, upon which he demanded my sword. I delivered it to him, and he brought me to prison. During the time I was pursued, I had many hair breadth escapes, which your [T. R. G.'s] time will not permit you to relate [write down]. I am here loaded with chains and willing to suffer the fate that awaits me.

[T. R. G.:] I here proceeded to make some inquiries of him—after assuring him of the certain death that awaited him, and that concealment would only bring destruction of the innocent as well as [the] guilty of his own color—if he knew of any extensive or concerted plan. His answer was, "I do not." When I questioned him as to the insurrection in North Carolina happening about the same time, he denied any knowledge of it; and when I looked him in the face as though I would search his inmost thoughts, he replied, "I see, sir, you doubt my word; but can you not think the same ideas, and strange appearances about this time in the heavens, might prompt others as well as myself to this undertaking?" I now had much conversation with and asked him many questions, having forborne to do so previously, except in the cases noted in parenthesis [changed to brackets here, with Gray's initials added]; but during his statement I had, unnoticed by him, taken notes as to some particular circumstances; and having the advantage of his statement before me in writing, on the evening of the third day that I had been with him I began a cross examination, and found his statement corroborated by every circumstance coming within my own knowledge or the confessions of others who had been either killed or executed, and whom he had not seen nor had any knowledge [of] since

22d of August last. He expressed himself fully satisfied as to the impracticality of his attempt. It has been said he was ignorant and cowardly, and that his object was to murder and rob for the purpose of obtaining money to make his escape. It is notorious that he was never known to have a dollar in his life, to swear an oath, or drink a drop of spirits. As to his ignorance, he certainly never had the advantages of education, but he can read and write (it was taught him by his parents), and for natural intelligence and quickness of apprehension is surpassed by few men I have ever seen. As to his being a coward, his reason as given for not resisting Mr. Phipps shews the decision of his character. When he saw Mr. Phipps present his gun, he said he knew it was impossible for him to escape as the woods were full of men; he therefore thought it was better to surrender and trust to fortune for his escape. He is a complete fanatic, or plays his part most admirably. On other subjects he possesses an uncommon share of intelligence, with a mind capable of attaining any thing but warped and perverted by the influence of early impressions. He is below the ordinary stature, though strong and active, having the true negro face, every feature of which is strongly marked. I shall not attempt to describe the effect of his narrative as told and commented on by himself in the condemned hole of the prison. The calm, deliberate composure with which he spoke of his late deeds and intentions—the expression of his fiend-like face when excited by enthusiasm—still bearing the stains of the blood of helpless innocence about him—clothed with rags and covered with chains, yet daring to raise his manacled hands to heaven, with a spirit soaring above the attributes of man—I looked on him and my blood curdled in my veins. . . .

Chapter Six

The Culmination of Northern Black Resistance

SECTION 1. RESISTANCE POETRY

Conditions of blacks both North and South, and individual acts of bravery and resistance, inspired and were reflected in the poetry of three free-born Negroes. "America," the first poem reprinted below, was written by James Whitfield, a barber and advocate of emigration to Central America, who published his *America, and Other Poems* in 1853. Frances Ellen Watkins, one of the most vigorous black female reformers, worked with the underground railroad in Little York, Pennsylvania, for a time and attended abolitionist meetings, often as a featured speaker, in almost all of the Northern states. After the war she became active in the Women's Christian Temperance Union. She published four books of poetry, the selection chosen being taken from her first volume, *Poems on Various Subjects* (1854). Dr. Martin R. Delany, a man of multiple talents, wrote and lectured widely for the abolitionist cause. In 1859 his poem, "Blake; or, the Huts of America," was printed in the black publication, *The Anglo-African Magazine*; that it shares some lines with "Sam's Song" (see Chapter III) is probably due to mutual inspiration from a traditional source. "Blake" is the last selection printed here.

Whitfield: America*

America, it is to thee,
Thou boasted land of liberty, —
It is to thee I raise my song,
Thou land of blood, and crime, and wrong.
It is to thee my native land,
From which has issued many a band
To tear the black man from his soil,
And force him here to delve and toil;
Chained on your blood-bemoistened sod,
Cringing beneath a tyrant's rod,
Stripped of those rights which Nature's God
   Bequeathed to all the human race,
Bound to a petty tyrant's nod,
   Because he wears a paler face.
Was it for this that freedom's fires
Were kindled by your patriot sires?
Was it for this they shed their blood,
On hill and plain, on field and flood?
Was it for this that wealth and life
Were staked upon that desperate strife,
Which drenched this land for seven long years
With blood of men, and women's tears?
When black and white fought side by side,
   Upon the well-contested field, —
Turned back the fierce opposing tide,
   And made the proud invader yield —
When, wounded, side by side they lay,
   And heard with joy the proud hurrah
From their victorious comrades say
   That they had waged successful war,
The thought ne'er entered in their brains
That they endured those toils and pains,
To forge fresh fetters, heavier chains
For their own children, in whose veins
Should flow that patriotic blood,
So freely shed on field and flood.

---

* The three selections in this section are reprinted from Sterling A. Brown, Arthur P. Davis, and Ulysses Lee, eds. *The Negro Caravan: Writings by American Negroes* (New York, 1941), pp. 290–291, 294–295, 447.

Oh, no; they fought, as they believed,
　For the inherent rights of man;
But mark, how they have been deceived
　By slavery's accursed plan.
They never thought, when thus they shed
　Their heart's best blood, in freedom's cause,
That their own sons would live in dread,
　Under unjust, oppressive laws:
That those who quietly enjoyed
　The rights for which they fought and fell,
Could be the framers of a code,
　That would disgrace the fiends of hell!
Could they have looked, with prophet's ken,
　Down to the present evil time,
　Seen free-born men, uncharged with crime,
Consigned unto a slaver's pen, —
Or thrust into a prison cell,
With thieves and murderers to dwell —
While that same flag whose stripes and stars
Had been their guide through freedom's wars
As proudly waved above the pen
Of dealers in the souls of men!
Or could the shades of all the dead,
　Who fell beneath that starry flag,
Visit the scenes where they once bled,
　On hill and plain, on vale and crag,
By peaceful brook, or ocean's strand,
　By inland lake, or dark green wood,
Where'er the soil of this wide land
　Was moistened by their patriot blood, —
And then survey the country o'er,
　From north to south, from east to west,
And hear the agonizing cry
Ascending up to God on high,
From western wilds to ocean's shore,
The fervent prayer of the oppressed;

And manhood, too, with soul of fire,
And arm of strength, and smothered ire,
Stands pondering with brow of gloom,
Upon his dark unhappy doom,

Whether to plunge in battle's strife,
And buy his freedom with his life,
And with stout heart and weapon strong,
Pay back the tyrant wrong for wrong
Or wait the promised time of God,
    When his Almighty ire shall wake,
And smite the oppressor in his wrath,
And hurl red ruin in his path,
And with the terrors of his rod,
    Cause adamantine hearts to quake.
Here Christian writhes in bondage still,
    Beneath his brother Christian's rod,
And pastors trample down at will,
    The image of the living God.

Almighty God! thy aid impart,
And fire anew each faltering heart,
And strengthen every patriot's hand,
Who aims to save our native land.
We do not come before thy throne,
    With carnal weapons drenched in gore,
Although our blood has freely flown,
    In adding to the tyrant's store.
Father! before thy throne we come,
    Not in panoply of war,
With pealing trump, and rolling drum,
    And cannon booming loud and far;
Striving in blood to wash out blood,
    Through wrong to seek redress for wrong;
For while thou'rt holy, just and good,
    The battle is not to the strong;
But in the sacred name of peace,
    Of justice, virtue, love and truth,
We pray, and never mean to cease,
    Till weak old age and fiery youth
In freedom's cause their voices raise,
And burst the bonds of every slave;
Till, north and south, and east and west,
The wrongs we bear shall be redressed.

Watkins: Eliza Harris

Like a fawn from the arrow, startled and wild,
A woman swept by us, bearing a child;
In her eye was the night of a settled despair,
And her brow was o'ershaded with anguish and care.

She was nearing the river—in reaching the brink,
She heeded no danger, she paused not to think;
For she is a mother—her child is a slave—
And she'll give him his freedom, or find him a grave!

It was a vision to haunt us, that innocent face—
So pale in its aspect, so fair in its grace;
As the tramp of the horse and the bay of the hound,
With the fetters that gall, were trailing the ground!

She was nerv'd by despair, and strengthened by woe,
As she leap'd o'er the chasms that yawn'd from below;
Death howl'd in the tempest, and rev'd in the blast,
But she heard not the sound till the danger was past.

Oh! how shall I speak of my proud country's shame?
Of the stains on her glory, how give them their name?
How say that her banner in mockery waves—
Her "star spangled banner"—o'er millions of slaves?

How say that the lawless may torture and chase
A woman whose crime is the hue of her face?
How the depths of the forest may echo around,
With the shrieks of despair, and the bay of the hound?

With her step on the ice, and her arm on her child,
The danger was fearful, the pathway was wild;
But, aided by Heaven, she gained a free shore,
Where the friends of humanity open'd their door.

So fragile and lovely, so fearfully pale,
Like a lily that bends to the breath of the gale,
Save the heave of her breast, and the sway of her hair,
You'd have thought her a statue of fear and despair.

In agony close to her bosom she press'd
The life of her heart, the child of her breast:—
Oh! love from its tenderness gathering might,
Had strengthen'd her soul for the dangers of flight.

But she's free!—yes, free from the land where the slave
From the hand of oppression must rest in the grave;
Where bondage and torture, where scourges and chains
Have plac'd on our banner indelible stains.

The bloodhounds have miss'd the scent of her way;
The hunter is rifled and foil'd of his prey;
Fierce jargon and cursing, with clanking of chains,
Make sounds of strange discord on Liberty's plains.

With the rapture of love and fulness of bliss,
She places on his brow a mother's fond kiss:—
O poverty, danger and death she can brave,
For the child of her love is no longer a slave!

Delany: Blake

Come all my brethren, let us take a rest,
While the moon shines bright and clear;
Old master died and left us all at last,
And has gone at the bar to appear!
Old master's dead and lying in his grave;
And our blood will now cease to flow;
He will no more tramp on the neck of the slave,
For he's gone where slave-holders go!
Hang up the shovel and the hoe-o-o-o!
I don't care whether I work or no!
    Old master's gone to the slave-holders rest—
He's gone where they all *ought* to go!

SECTION 2. INSTANCES OF PERSONAL ACTION

The two selections that begin this final chapter about the increasing
fervor of antislavery feeling among Northern blacks serve to illustrate

the fact that Southern slavery was not the only problem that faced the Negro in America.

If a black Northerner was permitted to attend a white church at all, he was most often required to sit apart in what was variously called "the African corner," "nigger Heaven," or "the nigger pew." Because of this insulting arrangement, many Negroes worshipped separately in their own churches, but on a few occasions black men decided to challenge the discrimination. The Reverend Jeremiah Asher wrote of one such "revolution" in his Hartford, Connecticut, Baptist church, and his ironic report is reprinted as the first document.

The second selection concerns a situation with more political significance. Robert Purvis of Philadelphia put long years of effort into Negro protest and resistance movements. Born free, in Charleston, South Carolina, he inherited a comfortable fortune from his English merchant father, and at the age of nine he moved to Philadelphia, afterwards obtaining his education in New England (including a short stay at Amherst College). He was one of the three Negroes present for the founding of the American Anti-Slavery Society in Philadelphia in 1833 and served almost continuously as one of its vice-presidents. Believing that black and white abolitionists should work together, the articulate and sarcastic Purvis made lecture tours for the Garrisonian-dominated organization, which was almost entirely white. In Philadelphia, Purvis was an active president of the General Vigilance Committee which sheltered large numbers of fugitive slaves, and also worked with other black leaders who pushed for the right of franchise. In 1853, enraged that part of his tax money was used to support schools that excluded Negroes, Purvis refused to make payment. Eventually, as the result of the active involvement of Purvis and others, township officials relented and Negro children were admitted to the schools.

Jeremiah Asher: the Pew Problem*

... I was advised to give up my determination, for such a course could not fail to bring me under the discipline of the church. However, I was immoveable; but the enquiry still was among the

---

* From Jeremiah Asher, *Incidents in the Life of the Rev. J. Asher, Pastor of Shiloh (Coloured) Baptist Church, Philadelphia, United States, and a Concluding Chapter of Facts Illustrating the Unrighteous Prejudice Existing in the Minds of American Citizens toward their Coloured Brethren* (London, 1850), pp. 43–47. Punctuation changed.

members of the church [as to] why I had left. I refused to give any information on the subject to any one except the deacons, and finally they communicated my reasons to some of the members; and the subject came up at a subsequent meeting for consideration, and instead of disciplining me they disciplined the Negro pews, for they [the pews] were arraigned and proved guilty of the charge of making distinction between the members of the body of Christ—condemned and excluded, never more to be admitted. This I regarded as a great triumph in behalf of my coloured brethren and sisters. But to my surprise, I was requested to meet a committee of the church to inform them what would satisfy the coloured members, for they were getting quite out of their place.

I informed these brethren in behalf of my coloured brethren and sisters, that the charge was not true—we were not at all difficult or hard to please. They asked nothing more than what had been already done; there was plenty of unoccupied seats in the gallery (I did not of course presume that black christians had a right to sit below in their Father's house) on either side; all we asked was to sit in the seats just as they were, without one penny expense by way of alteration. I contended that those seats which were made for whites were good enough for blacks; if they did not wish us to mix together, they could give us a certain number of seats expressly for coloured persons. But they were aware that without some visible distinction whites coming in would often be sitting in the Negro seat, and their devotions would be frequently disturbed by the pew-owner, who would be obliged to remove them and regulate all such irregularities. Hence they contended for the necessity of making considerable alterations, said it would be so much better and more respectable to make some nice seats of purpose for the coloured people. I said they were quite respectable and nice enough; we were quite willing to take sittings [reserved places] in them at the rate of those rented in the gallery; but if they were to be altered I must decline having anything to do with it—I should neither hire nor occupy one of them, even if they made them the best seats in the house; I would not pay for *proscription* any where, much less in the house of God, and especially in a Baptist Church, after having been welcome to all of the privileges of God's house in that place.

If men will disfranchise and separate from the rest of my Father's children, they shall do it at their own expense, not mine. I cannot prevent it, but I will not help them to do it. I will lift up my voice against it. However, my counsel was set aside and it was decided to make some nice seats on purpose for the coloured members; so they proceeded forthwith to carry this plan into execution. When finished, and an expense was incurred of about forty pounds, then it was noticed that these seats would be rented to the coloured people at one dollar a sitting per year. The time came, and I think there was not more than two or three [Negroes] present, and they did not take sittings. Now I was charged with preventing them, which certainly I did not. Matters came to such a crisis, I really thought I should be excluded; I was quite willing to be. At this time I did not attend any of the meetings for business. However, I received a very polite invitation to attend a meeting which was to be held in one of the coloured member's houses, in F. Street, when the pastor and deacons and all would be present and this troublesome matter must be settled. So I complied with this request and when the time came attended. I was called upon to open the meeting by prayer, which I at first declined; but as they urged it I tried to pray, and I learnt a lesson that day which I have not forgotten since: that is, to call upon God in the day of trouble. After prayer, the pastor presiding, began a kind of inquiry with the members, as to their objections to the nice little seats they had made them. All were inquired of before they interrogated me. I think there was not an objection raised. Then they inquired what I had to say, when I rose up from my seat and addressed them for about twenty or thirty minutes; and if ever I felt the presence of God, it was that day. I was not replied to either by the chair or any one of the assembly. It was agreed to report to the church favourably. The committee were satisfied; the coloured members might sit where they pleased in the galleries, and that was the end of this revolution.

Robert Purvis and the School Tax*

BYBERRY, Nov. 4th, 1853

MR. JOS. J. BUTCHER—*Dear Sir:* You called yesterday for the tax upon my property in this Township, which I shall pay, excepting the School Tax. I object to the payment of this tax on the ground that my rights as a citizen and my feelings as a man and a parent have been grossly outraged in depriving me, in violation of law and justice, of the benefits of the school system which this tax was

---

* From *The Liberator* (December 16, 1853); Some punctuation changes.

designed to sustain. I am perfectly aware that all that makes up the character and worth of the citizens of this township look upon the proscription and exclusion of my children from the Public School as illegal, and an unjustifiable usurpation of my right. I have borne this outrage ever since the innovation upon the usual practice of admitting *all* the children of the Township into the Public Schools, and at considerable expense have been obliged to obtain the services of private teachers to instruct my children while my school tax is greater, with a single exception, than that of any other citizen of the township. It is true (and the outrage is [thereby] made the more glaring and insulting) [that] I was informed by a *pious Quaker* director, with a sanctifying grace, imparting, doubt- less, an unctuous glow to his *saintly* prejudices, that a school in the village of Mechanicsville was appropriated for *"thine."* The miser- able shanty, with all its appurtenances, on the very line of the township, to which this benighted follower of George Fox alluded, is, as you know, the most flimsy and ridiculous sham which any tool of a skin-hating aristocracy could have resorted to, to cover or pro- tect his servility. To submit voluntary payment of the demand is too great an outrage upon nature, and, with a spirit, thank God, unshackled by this or any other wanton and cowardly act, I shall resist this tax, which before the unjust exclusion had always afforded me the highest gratification in paying. With no other than the best feelings towards yourself, I am forced to this unpleasant position, in vindication of my rights and personal dignity against an encroachment upon them as contemptibly mean as it is in- famously despotic.

Yours, very respectfully,

ROBERT PURVIS

SECTION 3.   TWO CRUCIAL CALLS TO ARMS

In the ante-bellum South, three men were regarded as the very incarnation of evil: Nat Turner, William Lloyd Garrison, and David Walker. Turner we have already met; Garrison, a leading white abolitionist, started *The Liberator* in 1831 (the year of Turner's revolt, for which he was blamed) and long maintained it as a major voice. Walker, the least-known of the three today, was like Turner a son of the South, born in 1785 in Wilmington, North Carolina, to a free mother and slave father. Believing that if he remained in the "bloody land," he would live only a short life, he journeyed to Boston where he became a dealer in clothing, old and new. He became actively involved in Negro causes. He was an agent for the abolitionist sheet, *Rights of All*, contributed money toward the purchase of George Horton, the black poet, and, in 1826, joined a Negro group dedicated to race advancement and the abolition of slavery. Privately, his comfortable home offered welcome respite from the "wretched" life black people were forced to endure.

After years of studying works of ancient and modern history and pondering Biblical teachings, Walker poured his knowledge and beliefs into a seventy-six-page pamphlet, *Walker's Appeal*, a powerful indictment of racism and slavery in the United States and a militant call to arms. His object, he wrote, was to arouse his "afflicted, degraded and slumbering brethren" to inquire into the sources of their wretchedness in this "Republican Land of Liberty." It was his own view that the causes were slavery, ignorance, misinterpretations of religion by white preachers, and the African colonization movement. Walker was convinced that God was just and that redemption for the black man was drawing near. He issued a warning to white America to change before it was too late: "Remember Americans, that we must and shall be free and enlightened as you are, will you wait until we shall, under God, obtain our liberty by the crushing arm of power? Will it not be dreadful for you? I speak Americans for your own good."

Walker predicted his words would provoke great criticism and would, perhaps, result in his death. Within a year following its publication, the pamphlet was out in a third edition. Northerners, abolitionists among them, condemned it; Southerners sought to suppress it. In the South, a thousand-dollar reward was offered for Walker's head, and ten times that amount if he were taken alive. Walker was arrested in Richmond in January, 1830, for distributing his work; however, he was permitted to return to Boston. A short time later, he died a sudden and still unexplained death.

The Reverend Henry Highland Garnet, like David Walker whom he admired, strongly voiced the rationale of black liberation. The grandson of a Mandingo chieftain, he was born on a plantation on the Eastern Shore of Maryland but when he was ten, his father, pretending to be driving his covered wagon to a funeral, succeeded in carrying his family and a few friends to Wilmington, Delaware, and freedom. Garnet received some education in New York City, and later attended Oneida

Institute, where he established a reputation as a good debater. Subsequently, under the tutelage of the Reverend Theodore Wright, one of the pioneer black abolitionists, he entered the ministry, becoming pastor of a Presbyterian church with a white congregation at Troy, New York, and quickly gained attention for his fiery denunciations of slavery. After an attempted kidnapping of his father, Garnet armed himself with a knife and announced his readiness to confront the slave-catcher should one come calling.

At the black national convention in Buffalo in 1843, twenty-seven-year-old Garnet delivered "An Address to the Slaves of the United States." In a more direct and forceful manner than Walker, Garnet called upon all slaves to strike for their lives and liberties if their masters refused to free them. "Rather *die freemen, than live to be slaves.*" The motion to adopt his "Address" was lost by but a single vote. Later, when abolitionist Maria Westen Chapman criticized him as an extremist, Garnet replied that he was only informing the country of what the "monster [slavery] has done, and is still doing." "Be assured," he wrote her, "that there is one black American who dares to speak boldly on the subject of universal liberty."

Five years later Garnet published *Walker's Appeal,* together with a laudatory biographical sketch, in a back-to-back edition with his own "Address." Black-emigration projects drew his energies in the 1850's, including, for a time, service as a missionary in Jamaica. He died in 1881 in Monrovia, Liberia.

Walker's Appeal, 1829*

. . . The whites want slaves, and want us for their slaves, but some of them will curse the day they ever saw us. As true as the sun ever shone in its meridian splendor, my colour will root some of them out of the very face of the earth. They shall have enough of making slaves of, and butchering, and murdering us in the manner which they have. No doubt some may say that I write with a bad spirit, and that I being a black, wish these things to occur. Whether I write with a bad or a good spirit, I say if these things do not occur

---

* From *Walker's Appeal, in Four Articles; together with a Preamble, to the Coloured Citizens of the World, but in Particular, and Very Expressly, to those of the United States of America,* written in Boston, State of Massachusetts, September 28, 1829; third and last edition, with additional notes, corrections, &c.; revised and published by David Walker (Boston, 1830). Slight changes in typography.

in their proper time, it is because...the world in which we live does not exist, and we are deceived with regard to its existence. It is immaterial, however, to me who believe or who refuse—though I should like to see the whites repent, peradventure God may have mercy on them; some, however, have gone so far that their cup must be filled.

...If you commence, make sure work—do not trifle, for they will not trifle with you—they want us for their slaves and think nothing of murdering us in order to subject us to that wretched condition—therefore, if there is an *attempt* made by us, kill or be killed. Now, I ask you, had you not rather be killed than to be a slave to a tyrant who takes the life of your mother, wife, and dear little children? Look upon your mother, wife, and children, and answer God Almighty! and believe this: that it is no more harm for you to kill a man who is trying to kill you than it is for you to take a drink of water when thirsty; in fact, the man who will stand still and let another murder him, is worse than an infidel and, if he has common sense, ought not to be pitied.

...What the American preachers can think of us, I aver this day before my God I have never been able to define. They have newspapers and monthly periodicals, which they receive in continual succession, but on the pages of which you will scarcely ever find a paragraph respecting slavery, which is ten thousand times more injurious to this country than all the other evils put together, and which will be the final overthrow of its government unless something is very speedily done for their cup is nearly full. Perhaps they will laugh at or make light of this; but I tell you Americans! that unless you speedily alter your course, *you* and your *Country are gone! ! ! ! ! !* For God Almighty will tear up the very face of the earth!!!

Will not that very remarkable passage of Scripture be fulfilled on Christian Americans? Hear it Americans!! "He that is unjust, let him be unjust still:—and he which is filthy, let him be filthy still: and he that is righteous, let him be righteous still: and he that is holy, let him be holy still." I hope that the Americans may hear, but I am afraid that they have done us so much injury, and are so firm in the belief that our Creator made us to be an inheritance to them forever, that their hearts will be hardened, so that their destruction may be sure. This language, perhaps, is too harsh for the American's delicate ears. But Americans! Americans!! I warn you in the name of the Lord (whether you will hear, or forbear) to repent and reform, or you are ruined!!!

. . . It appears as though they are bent only on daring God
Almighty to do his best—they chain and handcuff us and our
children and drive us around the country like brutes, and go into
the house of the God of justice to return him thanks for having
aided them in their infernal cruelties inflicted upon us. Will the
Lord suffer this people to go on much longer, taking his holy name
in vain? Will he not stop them, PREACHERS and all? O Americans!
Americans!! I call God—I call angels—I call men, to witness, that
your DESTRUCTION *is at hand* and will be speedily consummated unless you REPENT.

. . . Man, in all ages and all nations of the earth, is the same.
Man is a peculiar creature—he is the image of his God; though he
may be subjected to the most wretched condition upon earth, yet
the spirit and feeling which constitute the creature, man, can never
be entirely erased from his breast because God, who made him
after his own image, planted it in his heart; he cannot get rid of it.
The whites knowing this, they do not know what to do; they know
that they have done us so much injury, they are afraid that we,
being men and not brutes, will retaliate, and woe will be to them;
therefore that dreadful fear, together with an avaricious spirit and
the natural love in them to be called masters (which term we will
yet honour them with to their sorrow) bring them to the resolve
that they will keep us in ignorance and wretchedness as long as
they possibly can, and make the best of their time while it lasts.
Consequently they themselves (and not us) render themselves our
natural enemies, by treating us so cruel.

They keep us miserable now, and call us their property, but
some of them will have enough of us by and by—their stomachs
shall run over with us; they want us for their slaves, and shall
have us to their fill. We are all in the world together, I said above,
because we cannot help ourselves (*viz.*, we cannot help the whites
murdering our mothers and our wives) ; but this statement is in-
correct, for we *can* help ourselves; for if we lay aside abject servility and be determined to act like men and not brutes, the murderers among the whites would be afraid to show their cruel heads.
But O, my God!—in sorrow I must say it—that my colour all over
the world have a mean, servile spirit. They yield in a moment to
the whites, let them be right or wrong—the reason they are able
to keep their feet on our throats. Oh my coloured brethren, all over
the world, when shall we arise from this death-like apathy?—And
be men!! You will notice, if ever we become men (I mean *respect-*

able men such as other people are) we must exert ourselves to the full.

. . . Remember, Americans, that we must and shall be free and enlightened as you are. Will you wait until we shall under God obtain our liberty by the crushing arm of power? Will it not be dreadful for you? I speak, Americans, for your good. We must and shall be free, I say, in spite of you. You may do your best to keep us in wretchedness and misery to enrich you and your children, but God will deliver us from under you. And wo, wo will be to you if we have to obtain our freedom by fighting. Throw away your fears and prejudices, then, and enlighten us and treat us like men, and we will like you more than we do now hate you; and tell us now no more about colonization, for America is as much our country as it is yours.

. . . The Americans may say or do as they please, but they have to raise us from the condition of brutes to that of respectable men and to make a national acknowledgement to us for the wrongs they have inflicted on us. As unexpected, strange, and wild as these propositions may to some appear, it is no less a fact that unless they are complied with, the Americans of the United States, though they may for a little while escape, God will yet weigh them in a balance, and if they are not superior to other men, as they have represented themselves to be, he will give them wretchedness to their very heart's content.

Garnet's Address, 1843*

. . . Think how many tears you have poured out upon the soil which you have cultivated with unrequited toil and enriched with your blood; and then go to your lordly enslavers and tell them plainly that you *are determined to be free.* Appeal to their sense of justice, and tell them that they have no more right to oppress you than you have to enslave them. Entreat them to remove the grievous burdens which they have imposed upon you, and to remunerate you for your labor. Promise them renewed diligence in the cultivation of the soil, if they will render to you an equivalent for your services. Point

---

* From "An Address to the Slaves of the United States of America," in *A Memorial Discourse; by Rev. Henry Highland Garnet, delivered in the Hall of the House of Representatives, Washington . . . February 12, 1865, with an introduction by James McCune Smith* (Philadelphia, 1865), pp. 44–51. Punctuation changed.

them to the increase of happiness and prosperity in the British West Indies since the Act of Emancipation.

Tell them in language which they cannot misunderstand of the exceeding sinfulness of slavery, and of a future judgment, and of the righteous retributions of an indignant God. Inform them that all you desire is FREEDOM, and that nothing else will suffice. Do this, and for ever after cease to toil for the heartless tyrants, who give you no other reward but stripes and abuse. If they then commence the work of death, they, and not you, will be responsible for the consequences. You had better all die—*die immediately*—than live slaves and entail your wretchedness upon your posterity. If you would be free in this generation, here is your only hope. However much you and all of us may desire it, there is not much hope of redemption without the shedding of blood. If you must bleed, let it all come at once—rather *die freemen than live to be slaves....*

You will not be compelled to spend much time in order to become inured to hardships. From the first moment that you breathed the air of heaven, you have been accustomed to nothing else but hardships. The heroes of the American Revolution were never put upon harder fare than a peck of corn and a few herrings per week. You have not become enervated by the luxuries of life. Your sternest energies have been beaten out upon the anvil of severe trial. Slavery has done this to make you subservient to its own purposes; but it has done more than this—it has prepared you for any emergency. If you receive good treatment, it is what you could hardly expect; if you meet with pain, sorrow, and even death, these are the common lot of slaves.

Fellow men! Patient sufferers! behold your dearest rights crushed to the earth! See your sons murdered, and your wives, mothers, and sisters doomed to prostitution. In the name of the merciful God, and by all that life is worth, let it no longer be a debatable question whether it is better to choose *Liberty or death.*

In 1822, Denmark Veazie of South Carolina, formed a plan for the liberation of his fellow men. In the whole history of human efforts to overthrow slavery, a more complicated and tremendous plan was never formed. He was betrayed by the treachery of his own people, and died a martyr to freedom. Many a brave hero fell, but history, faithful to her high trust, will transcribe his name on the same monument with Moses, Hampden, Tell, Bruce, and Wallace, Toussaint L'Ouverture, Lafayette, and Washington. That tremendous movement shook the whole empire of slavery. The guilty soul-thieves were overwhelmed with fear. It is a matter of fact that at that time, and in consequence of the threatened revolution, the slave States talked strongly of emancipation. But they blew but one blast of the trumpet of freedom and then laid it aside. As these men became quiet, the slaveholders ceased to talk about emancipation; and now behold your condition today! Angels sigh over it, and humanity has long since exhausted her tears in weeping on your account!

The patriotic Nathaniel Turner followed Denmark Veazie. He was goaded to desperation by wrong and injustice. By despotism his name has been recorded on the list of infamy, and future generations will remember him among the noble and brave.

Next arose the immortal Joseph Cinque, the hero of the *Amistad.* He was a native African, and by the help of God he emancipated a whole ship-load of his fellow men of the high seas. And he now sings of liberty on the sunny hills of Africa and beneath his native palm-trees, where he hears the lion roar and feels himself as free as that king of the forest.

Next arose Madison Washington that bright star of freedom, and took his station in the constellation of true heroism. He was a slave on board the brig *Creole* of Richmond, bound to New Orleans, that great slave mart, with a hundred and four others. Nineteen struck for liberty or death. But one life was taken, and the whole were emancipated, and the vessel was carried into Nassau, New Providence.

Noble men! Those who have fallen in freedom's conflict, their memories will be cherished by the true-hearted and the God-fearing in all future generations; those who are living, their names are surrounded by a halo of glory.

Brethren, arise, arise! Strike for your lives and liberties. Now is the day and the hour. Let every slave throughout the land do this, and the days of slavery are numbered. You cannot be more oppressed than you have been—you cannot suffer greater cruelties than you have already. *Rather die freemen than live to be slaves.* Remember that you are FOUR MILLIONS!

It is in your power so to torment the God-cursed slaveholders that they will be glad to let you go free. If the scale was turned and black men were the masters and white men the slaves, every destructive agent and element would be employed to lay the oppressor low. Danger and death would hang over their heads day and night. Yes, the tyrants would meet with plagues more terrible than those of Pharoah. But you are a patient people. You act as though you were made for the special use of these devils. You act as though your daughters were born to pamper the lusts of your masters and overseers. And worse than all, you tamely submit while your lords tear your wives from your embraces and defile them before your eyes. In the name of God, we ask, are you men? Where is the blood of your fathers? Has it all run out of your veins? Awake, awake; millions of voices are calling you! Your dead fathers speak to you from their graves. Heaven, as with a voice of thunder, calls on you to arise from the dust.

Let your motto be resistance! *resistance!* RESISTANCE! No oppressed people have ever secured their liberty without resistance. What kind of resistance you had better make, you must decide by the circumstances that surround you and according to the suggestion of expediency. Brethren, adieu! Trust in the living God. Labor for the peace of the human race, and remember that you are FOUR MILLIONS.

SECTION 4. VOICES IN THE TURMOIL OF THE 1850's

It was in the fifties that the uncompromising attitudes of men like Walker and Garnet became common to the black resistance movement. Previously the laws of most states, though they forbade interference with the pursuers of escaped slaves, had not directly prevented citizens from helping them; the Fugitive Slave Act of 1850 now made it a federal offense to aid a runaway and put federal authorities in charge of returning suspected escapees to bondage without jury trial; of course, this also much increased the vulnerability of underground railroad activities.

Resistance meetings were staged all over the North following passage of the Fugitive Slave Act. Ad hoc groups passed resolutions denouncing the law and urging fugitives to arm themselves and resist unto death. Among the inspiriting individual orations were those delivered by two fugitive slaves, Samuel Ringgold Ward to a session in Boston, and John S. Jacobs at a black gathering in the Zion Church in New York City. Portions of their addresses are reprinted here.

Of Martin Delany, the free-born Harvard-trained physician, Frederick Douglass once remarked, "I thank God for making me a man

simple, but Delany always thanks Him for making him a black man."
In speeches and articles for his own newspaper the *Pittsburgh Mystery*
and later for Douglass's paper, Delany claimed for black people all the
rights of American citizens. By the early 1850's, however, the minute
progress of Negroes and the increasingly hostile atmosphere induced
Delany to decide that emigration was the only course for the black man.
Accordingly, he published a book in 1852 extolling the virtues of
Central America as a site for colonization, only to change his mind
later and journey to Africa where he signed a treaty with the Yoruba
tribe for a tract of land on which to settle black Americans. He also
migrated to Canada where he briefly practiced medicine in Chatham.
During the Civil War, Delany served as a major in the Union Army; and
at its close he moved to Charleston, South Carolina, where he became
involved in Reconstruction politics. In a letter to William Lloyd Garrison
on May 14, 1852, Delany explained his commitment to emigration: a
passage of the letter is reprinted next in this section.

By 1857 — the year in which the Supreme Court's Dred Scott
decision decreed that no black man was entitled to a citizen's rights —
many black militants had ceased to expect significant aid or comfort
from white society. Thus in that year Frederick Douglass, speaking in
Canandaigua, New York, at the twenty-third anniversary celebration of
the British abolition of slavery in the West Indies, eloquently argued
that the "progress of human liberty" would come only through struggle, and that the struggle must entail black resistance, both verbal and
physical.

A reprinted passage from Douglass's speech is followed by some
words, spoken at a Massachusetts Anti-Slavery Society meeting in the
same year, by the fiery black abolitionist, Charles Lenox Remond. Free-
born in Salem, Massachusetts, Remond early joined the antislavery
movement, becoming one of four representatives of the American Anti-
Slavery Society at the first world convention of abolitionists in London in
1840; while touring the British Isles, he publicly declared that he looked
forward to the United States and England's going to war over the Canadian boundary, since freedom for slaves would be a natural consequence.
A year later, back in this country, he indulged in hopeful speculation
that dissolution of the Union would unleash slaves on their masters.
With the black lawyer and civil rights activist, Robert Morris, he
appeared before the Massachusetts Military Committee with petitions
calling for the establishment of a Negro military company. The passage
reprinted here to close this section is one of Remond's most radical
pronouncements.

Samuel Ringgold Ward, 1850*

... The bill of which you most justly complain, concerning the surrender of fugitive slaves, is to apply alike to your State and to our State, if it shall ever apply at all. But we have come here to make a common oath upon a common altar, that that bill shall never take effect. (*Applause.*) Honorable Senators may record their names in its behalf, and it may have the sanction of the House of Representatives; but we, the people, who are superior to both Houses and the Executive, too—we, the people, will never be human bipeds, to howl upon the track of the fugitive slave. . . .

This is the question. Whether a man has a right to himself and his children, his hopes and his happiness, for this world and the world to come. That is a question which according to this bill may be decided by any backwoods postmaster in this State or any other. Oh, this is a monstrous proposition; and I do thank God that if the Slave Power has such demands to make on us, that the proposition has come now—now that the people know what is being done—now that the public mind is turned toward this subject—now that they are trying to find what is the truth on this subject. . . .

I am thankful that this, my first entrance into Boston . . . gives me the pleasure and privilege . . . of declaring in behalf of our people that if the fugitive slave is traced to our part of New York State, he shall have the law of Almighty God to protect him—the law which says, "Thou shalt not return to the master the servant that is escaped unto thee, but he shall dwell with thee in thy gates, where it liketh him best." And if our postmasters cannot maintain their constitutional oaths, and cannot live without playing the pander to the slave-hunter, they need not live at all. Such crises as these leave us the right of Revolution, and if need be that right we will, at whatever cost, most sacredly maintain.

John Jacobs, 1850†

John S. Jacobs, a fugitive, then came forward and spoke nearly as follows:—He said he came here tonight to give some advice and to extend the hand of fellowship to his colored brethren. He said:

---

* From *The Liberator* (April 5, 1850), with slightly changed typography.

† *National Anti-Slavery Standard* (October 10, 1850); punctuation slightly changed.

My colored brethren, if you have not swords, I say to you, sell your garments and buy one. He regretted that he was not in time to hear the resolutions read, to know if they were strong enough. If there be any man here tonight who wants to know my name, tell him it is John S. Jacobs, of South Carolina, and that I am an American citizen—that I never denied that name, neither did I ever disgrace it. They said that they cannot take us back to the South; but I say, under the present law they can; and now I say unto you, let them only take your dead bodies. (*Tremendous cheers.*) This is no time, my friends, to laugh; let us go to the house of mourning, and see the dead body of the wife of Hamlet and her surviving infants. Well, I would rather see her body dragged to the stake than to see her dragged back again into Slavery. I would, my friends, advise you to show a front to our tyrants and arm yourselves; aye, and I would advise the women to have their knives too. But I don't advise you to trample on this bill, and I further advise you to let us go on immediately, and act like men. He then advised the colored race to lay aside their religious and political feelings, or anything that may tend to separate them, and suggested that a registry should be commenced with the name of every slave, his owner, and all other particulars, that they might tend to give him every assistance, and concluded by advising the fugitives not to suffer themselves to be taken.

Delany for Emigration, 1852*

... I am not in favor of caste, nor a separation of the brotherhood of mankind, and would as willingly live among white men as black if I had an *equal possession and enjoyment* of privileges; but shall never be reconciled to live among them subservient to their will—existing by mere *sufferance* as we, the colored people, do in this country. The majority of white men cannot see why colored men cannot be satisfied with their condition in Massachusetts— what they desire more than the *granted* right of citizenship. Blind selfishness on the one hand and deep prejudice on the other will not permit them to understand that we desire the *exercise* and *enjoyment* of these rights, as well as the *name* of their possession. If there were any probability of this, I should be willing to remain

* Martin R. Delany to William Lloyd Garrison, May 14, 1852; in *The Liberator* (May 21, 1852); punctuation altered.

in the country, fighting and struggling on, the good fight of faith. But I must admit that I have no hopes in this country—no confidence in the American people—with a *few* excellent exceptions— therefore I have written as I have done. Heathenism and Liberty, before Christianity and Slavery.

> Where I a slave, I would be free
> I would not live to live a slave;
> But boldly *strike* for LIBERTY—
> For FREEDOM or a *Martyr's* grave

Douglass: Struggle Is Necessary, 1857*

Let me give you a word of the philosophy of reform. The whole history of the progress of human liberty shows that all concessions yet made to her august claims have been born of earnest struggle. This conflict has been exciting, agitating, all-absorbing, and for the time being putting all other tumults to silence. It must do this or it does nothing. If there is no struggle, there is no progress. Those who profess to favor freedom and yet deprecate agitation are men who want crops without plowing up the ground; they want rain without thunder and lightning. They want the ocean without the awful roar of its many waters.

This struggle may be a moral one, or it may be a physical one, or it may be both moral and physical, but it must be a struggle. Power concedes nothing without a demand. It never did, and it never will. Find out just what any people will quietly submit to, and you have found out the exact measure of injustice and wrong which will be imposed upon them, and these will continue till they are resisted with either words or blows, or with both. The limits of tyrants are prescribed by the endurance of those whom they oppress. In the light of these ideas, Negroes will be hunted at the North, and held and flogged at the South, so long as they submit to those devilish outrages and make no resistance, either moral or physical. Men may not get all they pay for in this world; but they must certainly pay for all they get. If we ever get free from all the oppressions and wrongs heaped upon us, we must pay for their removal. We must do this by labor, by suffering, by sacrifice, and, if needs be, by our lives and the lives of others.

---

* From Philip S. Foner, *The Life and Writings of Frederick Douglass*, vol. 2 (New York, 1950), p. 437, with some changes in punctuation.

Charles Lenox Remond, 1857*

... I ask you if I say too much when I say that to the slave the popular Fourth of July in the United States is an insult? ... The time is coming when a larger number than is gathered here today will subscribe to the idea of the dissolution of the Union as the only means of their own safety, as well as of the emancipation of the slave. ...

Sir, I do not care, so far as I am concerned, to view even the deeds committed by the greatest men of the Revolution, nor the purposes which they achieved. ... I do know, in my heart, that every slave on every plantation has the right from his God and Creator to be free, and that is enough to warrant me in saying that we cannot come here for a better or a nobler purpose than to help forward the effort to dissolve the American Union; because if the Union shall be dissolved, if for no other purpose than for the emancipation of the slave, it will be glory enough for me to engage in it.

I ... speak for myself; and in doing so I speak and determine for the freedom of every slave on every plantation, and for the fugitives on my right hand; and in so speaking I speak for those before me as emphatically as I can for the blackest man that lives or suffers in our country. ... I have not a word to say about the evils of American slavery as they are detailed on the one hand, and retailed on the other. The time has come for us to make the ground upon which we stand today sacred to the cause of liberty; and when we make the ground of Framingham thus sacred, we do away with the necessity for the disgraceful underground railroad of our country that transports such men as these fugitives to the dominions of the British Queen in order that they may secure their alienable rights; we do away with the dishonor that now gathers around and over the State of Massachusetts which makes it necessary for any man or any woman to pass beyond our border before he or she can be free. Talk to me of Bunker Hill, and tell me that a fugitive passed through Boston today! Talk about Lexington, and tell me a slave mother must be kept secreted in Boston! Talk to me of commemorating the memory of Joseph Warren while 30,000 fugitive slaves are in Canada! I will scout the memory of the Revolution, the memory of Washington, and Adams, and Hancock, until the soil of Massachusetts shall be as free to every fugitive, and as free

---

* *The Liberator* (July 10, 1857); punctuation changed.

to me, as it is to the descendants of any one of them. And until we shall do this, we talk in vain, and celebrate in vain.

. . . I am not the man to speak to a white audience on the Fourth of July. I am reminded by everything over me, beneath me, and all around me, of my shame and degradation; and I shall take my seat on this occasion by stating to every white man present, who does not feel that the time has come when the rights of the colored man should be restored to him, that I am among the number who would embrace this day, this moment, to strike the last fetter from the limbs of the last slave, if it were in my power to do so, and leave the consequences to those at whose instigation it has been fastened upon them.

I look around the country and behold one other demonstration, and with the mention of that, I shall take my seat. . . . The election of James Buchanan to the presidency has placed that question beyond doubt and cavil and has determined that the American people, by an overwhelming majority, are on the side of slavery with all its infernalism. Now, Sir, it belongs to the true friends who are present to go forward determined that this state of things shall be altered; and it can only be altered by the largest application and the freest promulgation of the doctrine set forth by the American and Massachusetts Anti-Slavery Societies. I am glad, therefore, to utter my testimony from a platform where they are represented; and let me say, friends, whether you believe it or not, that if the cause of universal liberty shall ever be established in our country, within our day and generation, it can only be by the promulgation to the country of the most radical type of antislavery. . . .

SECTION 5. MILITANT ACTION

The documents reprinted in this section show that the increasing pre-war militancy was not confined to stirring speeches.

Organizations to aid fugitive slaves, frequently called vigilance committees, which were staffed predominately, if not entirely, by Negroes, operated in a number of strategically located cities and towns in the North. In 1845 a group of black men and women, led by such persons as Henry Weeden and William C. Nell, formed the New England

Freedom Association. Although their purpose was illegal, their approach was forthright. The announcement of their intentions in William Lloyd Garrison's antislavery newspaper, *The Liberator,* is the first reprinted document.

From within the Negro ranks, an occasional betrayer came forward to claim his "thirty pieces of silver" by turning over fugitives to the authorities or to agents of the slaveowners. The Negro press regularly listed the names of informers, some of whom were severely punished by other Negroes, being beaten or tarred and feathered. In August of 1858 one John Brodie, on the promise of three hundred dollars from slaveowners, betrayed two fugitive slaves. The action and its consequences are related in a reprinted letter from William C. Nell to William Lloyd Garrison.

Charles Langston, brother of the prominent lawyer and educator John Mercer Langston, was a remarkable man in his own right. One of the first two Negroes admitted to Oberlin College (in the Preparatory Department, along with another brother, Gideon Langston), Charles worked as a school teacher and dentist. As a leading participant in the Ohio state black convention movement of the 1850's, Charles Langston was active in both civil rights and antislavery activities. At the 1851 Ohio convention he called on every slave from "Maryland to Texas, to arise and assist their Liberties, and cut their masters' throats if they attempt again to reduce them to slavery." In 1858 Langston took part in the Oberlin-Wellington rescue of fugitive John Price from a party that included two deputy U.S. marshals. Thirty-seven men, twelve of them Negro, were indicted but only two, Simeon Bushnell (a white Oberlin resident) and Charles Langston, were brought to trial. When he was permitted to address the court, Langston made a stinging indictment of the prejudices of white America, especially as expressed in the Fugitive Slave Law, and an inspiring plea for the dignity of man. He received a light sentence: twenty days in jail and a fine of one hundred dollars. His address to the court is printed next in order.

One of the most famous of all attempts to start a Southern slave insurrection was made by the radical white abolitionist John Brown, variously called a madman and an agent of divine will. In the autumn of 1859, Brown and eighteen of his followers made an ill-fated attack on the government's arsenal at Harpers Ferry, Virginia. Among the five Negroes who accompanied Brown was the youthful John A. Copeland, Jr., an Oberlin carpenter and one-time student in the Oberlin College Preparatory Department. Prior to his execution, Copeland wrote a letter to his family, a portion of which concludes this section.

The New England Freedom Association*

The object of our Association is to extend a helping hand to all who may bid adieu to whips and chains, and by the welcome light of the North Star reach a haven where they can be protected from the grasp of the man-stealer. An article of the constitution enjoins upon us not to pay one farthing to any slaveholder for the property they may claim in a human being. We believe that to be the appropriate work of those at the North who contend that the emancipation of the slaves should be preceded by the compensation of the masters. Our mission is to succor those who claim property in themselves, and thereby acknowledge an independence of slavery.

Fugitives are constantly presenting themselves for assistance which we are at times unable to afford, in consequence of the lack of means. Donations of money or clothing, information of places where they may remain for a temporary or permanent season as the case may demand — these are the instrumentalities by which we aim to effect our object. We feel it to be a legitimate branch of anti-slavery duty, and solicit, therefore, in the name of the panting fugitive, the countenance and support of all who "remember those in bonds as bound with them." . . . Donations are punctually acknowledged in some of the anti-slavery papers.

Punishing a Slave-Betrayer†

. . . Rev. Mr. Davis, Chairman, then introduced Rev. H. H. Garnet, who in a graphic and eloquent manner detailed the history of the kidnapping case, tracing [John] Brodie's connection with it under written instructions from the slaveholders, until the imprisonment of the two captives in the jail at Covington, Ky. They [the fugitives] had accepted Brodie's pledge to assist their return to the South with a view to secure the liberation of some of their relatives from slavery. Instead of this blissful realization of their hopes, they were delivered into the hands of their self-styled owners, and by the very man in whom they had most implicitly trusted (receiving each one hundred lashes), and ordered to be sold further South expressly to cut off all future chance of escape to the North. Mr. Garnet exhibited a pair of manacles, such

---

* From *The Liberator* (December 12, 1845) ; punctuation altered.
† From *The Liberator* (September 11, 1858).

as were worn by them on their way to jail, and a bull whip, as
used in their severe flogging.

The young men of Cincinnati on learning the facts, with that
"eternal vigilance" which is "the price of liberty," succeeded in
getting possession of the traitor and instituted measures for his
trial. This occupied two hours, during most of which time Mr.
Garnet was present, and it was mainly owing to his intercession
that Brodie was not torn limb from limb. He escaped with life,
after the infliction of three hundred blows with a paddle — one
blow for each dollar of blood money which he had received for
doing the infamous work of these Kentucky hunters of men. Two
white men, in sympathy with the right though pretending otherwise to him, acted as police men and removed him from immediate
danger of being killed. He breathed vengeance upon the colored
people, threatened to expose the operations of the Underground
Railroad, etc., etc.; but when a committee of colored men started
for the purpose of hurrying him from Cincinnati, it was found
that his gold had bribed the white men who were endeavoring to
screen him from further molestation. But the colored men were
determined, and his whereabouts was made known. Brodie delivered himself into the hands of the authorities, who put him in
jail to save his life.

Langston: The Oberlin–Wellington Rescue[*]

I am for the first time in my life before a court of Justice
charged with the violation of law, and am now about to be sentenced. But before receiving that sentence, I propose to say one
or two words in regard to the mitigation of that sentence, if it
may be so construed. I cannot, of course, and do not, expect [that]
that which I may say will in any way change your predetermined
line of action. I ask no such favor at your hands.

I know that the courts of this country, that the laws of this
country, that the governmental machinery of this country, are so
constituted as to oppress and outrage colored men, men of my
complexion. I cannot then, of course, expect, judging from the past
history of the country, any mercy from the laws, from the constitution, or from the courts of the country.

---

[*] Charles Langston, quoted by John Mercer Langston, "The Oberlin–
Wellington Rescue," *Anglo-American Magazine* (July, 1859), pp. 209–216;
changes made in punctuation.

Some days prior to the 13th day of September, 1858, happening to be in Oberlin on a visit, I found the country round about there and the village itself filled with alarming rumors as to the fact that slave-catchers, kidnappers, Negro-stealers were lying hidden and skulking about, waiting some opportunity to get their bloody hands on some helpless and life-long [victim of] bondage. These reports becoming current all over that neighborhood, old men and innocent women and children became exceedingly alarmed for their safety. It was not uncommon to hear mothers say that they dare not send their children to school for fear they would be caught and carried off by the way. Some of these people had become free by long and patient toil at night, after working the long, long day for cruel masters, and thus at length getting money enough to buy their liberty. Others had become free by the good will of their masters. And there were others who had become free by the intensest exercise of their God-given powers — by escaping from the plantations of their masters, eluding the bloodthirsty patrols and sentinels so thickly scattered all along their path, outrunning blood-hounds and horses, swimming rivers and fording swamps, and reaching at last, through incredible difficulties, what they in their delusion supposed to be free soil. These three classes were in Oberlin, trembling alike for their safety, because they well knew their fate should those men-hunters get their hands on them.

In the midst of such excitement the 13th day of September was ushered in — a day ever to be remembered in the history of that place, and I presume no less in the history of this Court — on which those men by lying devices decoyed into a place where they could get their hands on him — I will not say *a slave,* for I do not know that — but a *man,* a *brother,* who had a right to his liberty under the laws of God, under the laws of Nature, and under the Declaration of American Independence.

In the midst of all this excitement, the news came to us like a flash of lightning that an actual seizure, under and by means of fraudulent pretenses, had been made!

Being identified with that man by color, by race, by manhood, by sympathies such as God had implanted in us all, I felt it my duty to go and do what I could toward liberating him. I had been taught by my Revolutionary father — and I say this with all due respect to him — and by his honored associates, that the fundamental doctrine of this government was that *all* men have a right to life and liberty, and coming from the Old Dominion [Virginia] I brought into Ohio these sentiments deeply impressed upon my heart; I went to Wellington, and hearing from the parties themselves by what authority the boy was held in custody, I conceived from what little knowledge I had of law that they had no right to hold him. And as your Honor has repeatedly laid down the law in the Court, a man is free until he is proven to be legally restrained of his liberty, and I believed that upon the principle of law those men were bound to take their prisoner before the very first magistrate they found and there establish the facts set forth in their warrant — and that until they did this, every man should presume that their claim was unfounded — and [they were bound] to institute such proceedings for the purpose of securing an investigation as they might find warranted by the laws of this State. Now, sir, if that is not the plain, common sense and correct view of the law, then I have been misled by your Honor, and by the prevalent received opinion.

It is said that they had a warrant. Why then should they not establish its validity before the proper officers? And I stand here to-day, sir, to say that with an exception of which I shall soon speak, *to procure such a lawful investigation of the authority under which they claimed to act was the part I took in that day's proceedings, and the only part.* I supposed it to be my duty as a citizen of Ohio — excuse me for saying that, sir: as an *outlaw of the United States (Much sensation.)* — to do what I could to secure at least this form of Justice to my brother whose liberty was in peril. *Whatever more than that has been sworn to in this trial as an act of mine is false, ridiculously false.* When I found these men refusing to go, according to the law as I apprehended it, and subject their claim to an official inspection, and [found] that nothing short of a *habeas corpus* would oblige such an inspection, I was willing to go even thus far, supposing in that county a Sheriff might perhaps be found with nerve enough to serve it. In this I again failed. Nothing then was left me — nothing to the boy in custody — but the confirmation of my first belief that the pretended authority was worthless, and the employment of those means of liberation which belong to us. With regard to the part I took in the forcible rescue which followed I have nothing to say further than I have already said. The evidence is before you. It is alleged that I said, "We will have him anyhow." *This I never said.* I did say to Mr. Lowe what I honestly believed to be the truth: that the crowd was very much excited, many of them averse to longer delay and bent upon a rescue at all hazards, and that he being an old acquaintance and friend of mine, I was anxious to

extricate him from the dangerous position he occupied and therefore advised that he urge Jennings to give the boy up. Further
than this I did not say, either to him or any one else.

The law under which I am arraigned is an unjust one — one
made to crush the colored man, and one that outrages every feeling
of humanity as well as every rule of right. I have nothing to do
with its constitutionality; about that I care but little. I have often
heard it said by learned and good men that it was unconstitutional;
I remember the excitement that prevailed throughout all the free
States when it was passed; and I remember how often it has been
said by individuals, conventions, legislatures, and even *Judges*, that it
never could be, never should be, and never was meant to be enforced.
I had always believed, until contrary appeared in the actual institution of proceedings, that the provisions of this odious statute
would never be enforced within the bounds of this State.

But I have another reason to offer why I should not be sentenced, and one that I think pertinent to the case. I have not had
a trial before a jury of my peers. The common law of England —
and you will excuse me for referring to that, since I am but a
private citizen — was that every man should be tried before a jury
of men occupying the same position in the social scale with himself.
That lords should be tried before a jury of lords; that peers of the
realm should be tried before peers of the realm; vassals before
vassals, and *aliens before aliens*, and they must not come from the
district where the crime was committed, lest the prejudices of
either personal friends or foes should affect the accused. The
Constitution of the United States guarantees, not merely to its
citizens but *to all persons*, a trial before an *impartial* jury. I have
had no such trial.

The colored man is oppressed by certain universal and deeply
fixed *prejudices*. Those jurors are well known to have shared
largely in these prejudices, and I therefore consider that they were
neither impartial nor were they a jury of my peers. . . .

I was tried by a jury who were prejudiced before a Court that
was prejudiced, prosecuted by an officer who was prejudiced, and
defended, though ably, by counsel that were prejudiced. And therefore it is, your Honor, that I urge by all that is good and great in
manhood that I should not be subjected to the pains and penalties
of this oppressive law, when I have *not* been tried either by a jury
of my peers or by a jury that were impartial.

One more word, sir, and I have done. I went to Wellington
knowing that colored men have no rights in the United States

which white men are bound to respect; that the Courts had so decided; that Congress had so enacted; that the people had so decreed.

There is not a spot in this wide country, not even by the altars of God, nor in the shadow of the shafts that tell the imperishable fame and glory of the heroes of the Revolution — no, nor in the old Philadelphia Hall — where any colored man may dare to ask a mercy of a white man. Let me stand in that Hall and tell a United States Marshal that my father was a Revolutionary soldier — that he served under Lafayette and fought through the whole war, and that he fought for *my* freedom as much as for his own — and he would sneer at me and clutch me with his bloody fingers, and say he has a *right* to make me a slave! And when I appeal to Congress, they say he has a right to make me a slave; when I appeal to your Honor, *your Honor* says he has a right to make me a slave; and if any man, white or black, seeks an investigation of that claim, they make themselves amenable to the pains and penalties of the Fugitive Slave Act, for *BLACK MEN HAVE NO RIGHTS WHICH WHITE MEN ARE BOUND TO RESPECT.* *(Great applause.)* I, going to Wellington with the full knowledge of all this, knew that if that man was taken to Columbus he was hopelessly gone, no matter whether he had ever been in slavery before or not. I knew that I was in the same situation myself and that, by the decision of your Honor, if any man whatever were to claim me as his slave and seize me, and my brother (being a lawyer) should seek to get out a writ of *habeas corpus* to expose the falsity of the claim, he would be thrust into prison under one provision of the Fugitive Slave Law, for interfering with the man claiming to be in pursuit of a fugitive, and I, by the perjury of a solitary wretch, would by another of its provisions be helplessly doomed to life-long bondage, without the possibility of escape.

Some may say that there is no danger of free persons being seized and carried off as slaves. No one need labor under such a delusion. Sir, *four* of the eight persons who were first carried back under the act of 1850 were afterwards proved to be *free men.* They were free persons, but wholly at the mercy of the oath of one man. And but last Sabbath afternoon, a letter came to me from a gentleman in St. Louis informing me that a young lady who was formerly under my instructions at Columbus, a free person, is now lying in the jail at that place, claimed as the slave of some wretch who never saw her before and waiting for testimony from relatives at Columbus to establish her freedom. I could stand here by the hour and relate such instances. In the very nature of the case they must be constantly occurring. A letter was not long since found upon the person of a counterfeiter when arrested, addressed to him by some Southern gentleman, in which the writer says:

"Go among the Negroes; find out their marks and scars; make good descriptions and send to me, and I'll find masters for 'em."

That is the way men are carried "back" to slavery.

But in view of all the facts, I say that if ever again a man is seized near me and is about to be carried southward as a slave before any legal investigation has been had, I shall hold it to be my duty, as I held it that day, to secure for him if possible a legal inquiry into the character of the claim by which he is held. And I go further: I say that if it is adjudged illegal to procure even such an investigation, then we are thrown back upon those last defences of our rights which cannot be taken from us and which God gave us: that we need not be slaves. I ask your Honor while I say this to place yourself in my situation, and you will say with me that if your brother, if your friend, if your wife, if your child had been seized by men who claimed them as fugitives, and the law of the land forbade you to ask any investigation and precluded the possibility of any legal protection or redress — then you will say with me that you would not only demand the protection of the law, but you would call in your neighbors and friends and would ask them to say with you that these, your friends, *could not* be taken into slavery.

And now I thank you for this leniency, this indulgence, in giving a man unjustly condemned by a tribunal, before which he is declared to have no rights, the privilege of speaking in his own behalf. I know that it will do nothing towards mitigating your sentence, but it is a privilege to be allowed to speak and I thank you for it. I shall submit to the penalty, be it what it may. But I stand here to say that if, for doing what I did on that day at Wellington, I am to go in jail six months and pay a fine of a thousand dollars, according to the Fugitive Slave Law — and such is the protection the laws of this country afford me — I must take upon myself the responsibility of self-protection; when I come to be claimed by some perjured wretch as his slave, I shall never be taken into slavery. And as in that trying hour I would have others do to me, as I would call upon my friends to help me — as I would call upon you, your Honor, to help me, as I would call upon you *(to the District Attorney)* to help me, and upon you *(to Judge*

Bliss), and upon you *(to his counsel)* — *so help me God* I stand
here to say that I will do all I can for any man thus seized and
held, though the inevitable penalty of six months' imprisonment
and one thousand dollars fine for each offence hangs over me!
We have all a common humanity, and you all would do that; your
manhood would require it, and no matter what the laws might be
you would honor yourself for doing it, while your friends and your
children to all generations would honor you for doing it and every
good and honest man would say you had done right!

Copeland: a Negro with John Brown*

I am not terrified by the gallows, which I see staring me in the
face and upon which I am soon to stand and suffer death for doing
what George Washington was made a hero for doing. . . . For
having lent my aid to a general no less brave and engaged in a
cause no less honorable and glorious, I am to suffer death. Washington entered the field to fight for the freedom of the American
people — not for the white man alone, but for both black and
white. Nor were they white men alone who fought for the freedom
of this country. The blood of black men flowed as freely as that
of white men. . . . And some of the very last blood shed was that
of black men. . . . It was a sense of the wrongs which we have
suffered that prompted the noble but unfortunate Captain Brown
and his associates to attempt to give freedom to a small number,
at least, of those who are now held by cruel and unjust laws, and
by no less cruel and unjust men. . . . And now, dear brother, could
I die in a more noble cause? Could I die in a manner and for a
cause which would induce true and honest men more to honor me,
and the angels more ready to receive me to their happy home of
everlasting joy above? I imagine that I hear you, and all of you —
mother, father, sisters, and brothers — say — "No, there is not
a cause for which we, with less sorrow, could see you die." Believe
me when I tell you that, though shut up in prison and under sentence of death, I have spent many very happy hours here, and were
it not that I know that the hearts of those to whom I am attached
. . . will be filled with sorrow, I would almost as lief die now as at
any time, for I feel that I am now prepared to meet my Maker. . . .

---

* John A Copeland, quoted in Richard J. Hinton, *John Brown and His Men*
(New York, 1968), p. 509; punctuation altered.